AF580261

MONET

The Gardener

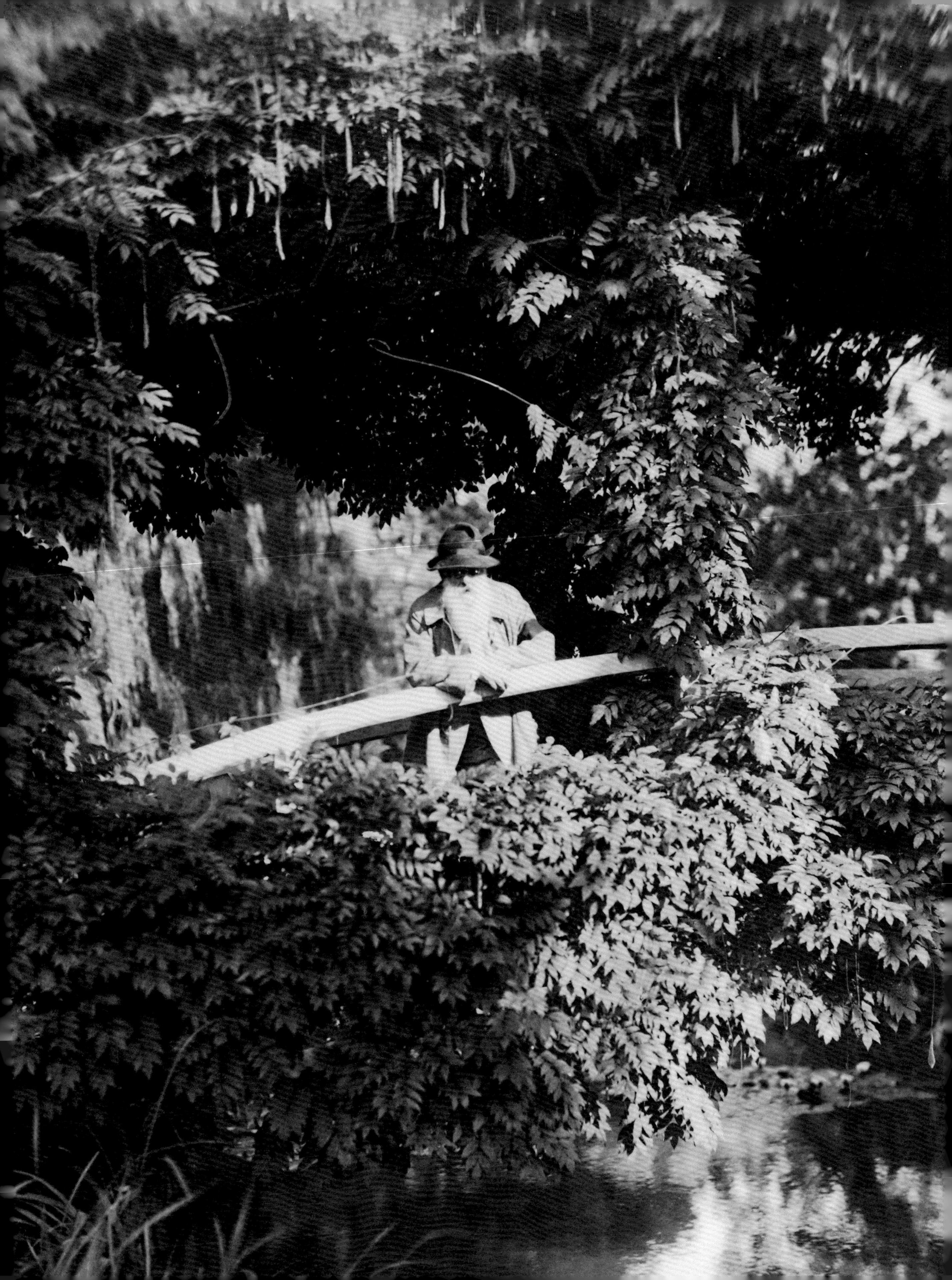

MONET
The Gardener

The Flowering Domain by Robert Gordon

A Gardening Life by Sydney Eddison

UNIVERSE

First published in the United States of America in 2002
by UNIVERSE PUBLISHING
A Division of Rizzoli International Publications, Inc.
300 Park Avenue South
New York, NY 10010

Prepared and produced by Constance Sullivan / Hummingbird Books
Designed by Christine N. Moog, Little Spoons Inc.

Printed and bound by L. E G. O.
Separations by Stampa Digitale

2002 2003 2004 2005 2006 / 10 9 8 7 6 5 4 3 2 1

Printed in Italy

Library of Congress Catalog Control Number: 2002110660

CONTENTS

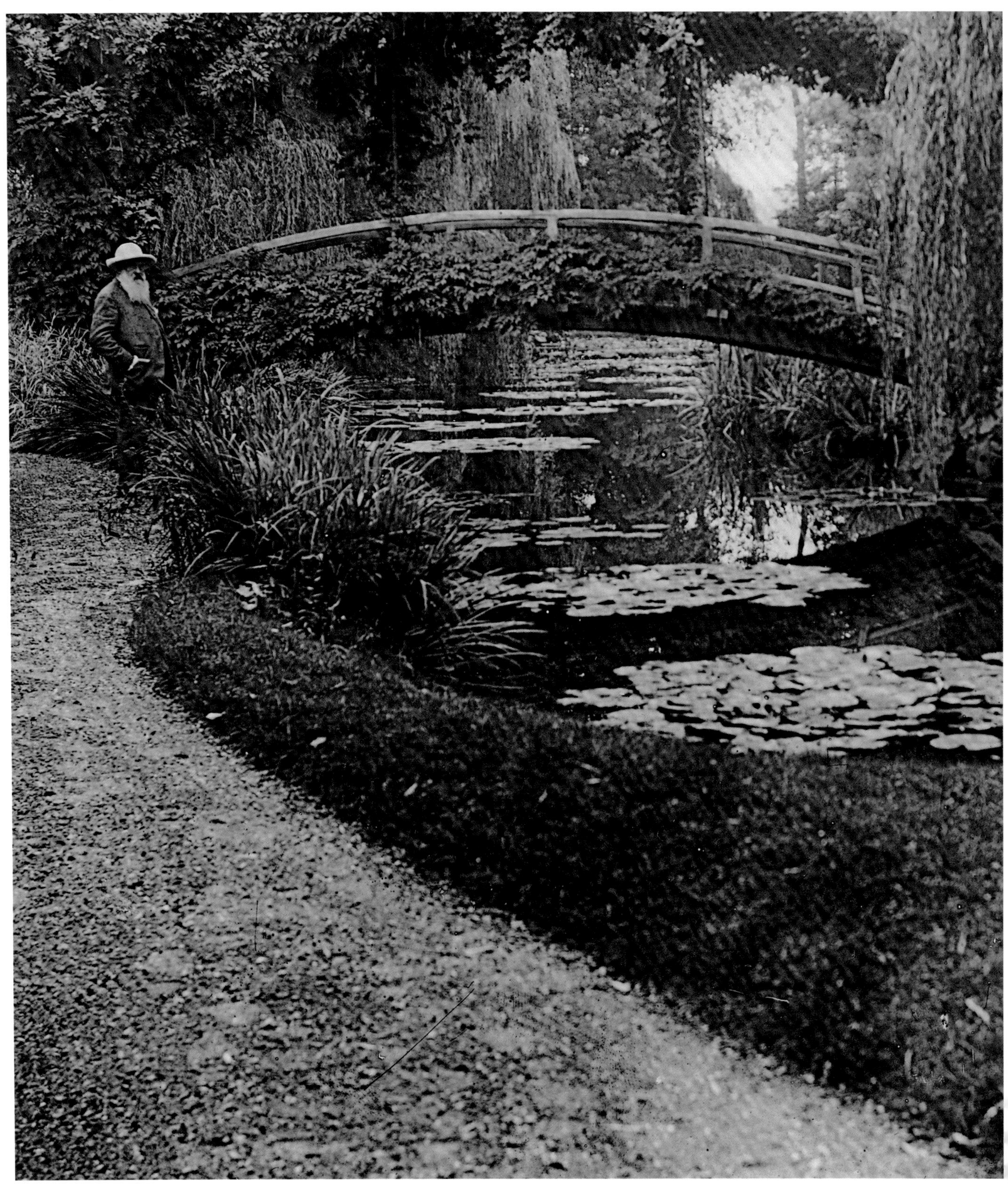

THE FLOWERING DOMAIN *Robert Gordon*

Monet's garden at Giverny resulted from the unique and highly personal combination of a painter's eye and a gardener's passion. His luxurious floral world was never static, but rather an ever-changing response to the pattern of colors and plants that he observed from one year to the next, and the desire to alter the garden's texture and allure in the seasons to come. Extremely disciplined and something of a tyrant, Monet structured his life to the requirements of his painting, organized his family life to coincide with his seasonal timetables, and was constantly preoccupied with ameliorations to his garden. As soon as he had resources to employ a team of gardeners to tend the property, he strictly supervised their efforts. A beautiful garden does not just happen. It demands extensive planning and constant maintenance. Monet's garden became more than a garden. It was his world, his home, and his most prized studio. Ultimately, it was the sole painting motif for the last two decades of his life.

It was in May 1883 that Monet and his family moved to Giverny, a farming village about fifty miles west of Paris, in the valley of the Seine at the border between the Île-de-France and Normandy. From the hillside overlooking the village, one could see vineyards; orchards of plum, apple, cherry, peach, and pear trees; abundant crops, vegetation, and several varieties of trees planted by local farmers and nurserymen; and the Seine sparkling with sunlight, at times divided by small islands, or dotted with barges and river traffic. Despite its relative proximity to Paris, it was definitely the country, and the Normans—not known for their hospitality—looked at this artist and his family with a mixture of curiosity and wariness.

Monet rented a large, though banal, house with a sizable garden from one of the leading Giverny landowners, Louis-Joseph Singeot. The most luxurious feature of the property was the wealth of trees distributed throughout. A central alleyway descended from the front door of the house to the main gate. The alley was crowned by two majestic yews at the house, and fir trees, particularly cypress and spruce, flanked the path on either side. The rest of the garden was mainly an orchard with many old and good fruit-bearing trees, while adjacent to the house was a grove of linden trees planted in the form of a horseshoe.

The garden required immediate tending, a task that Monet carried out with the aid of the older children from his and his future wife Alice's families. Vegetables were cultivated. In the first few years, the garden was a time-consuming chore, with a great deal of effort expended turning the

This photograph of the water-lily pond was taken near the spot where Monet painted the 1899–1900 series of works with the Japanese footbridge as their central element. In 1901 he began the series of excavations that would greatly enlarge the garden and permit a majestic panoply for the cultivation of water lilies. By 1923, the approximate date of this image, he had achieved his vision. But it was a private world: the water garden was sealed off by a railroad track that stopped most visitors, a series of fences that locked out everyone, and a wealth of roses and vines that discreetly guarded and concealed the interior.

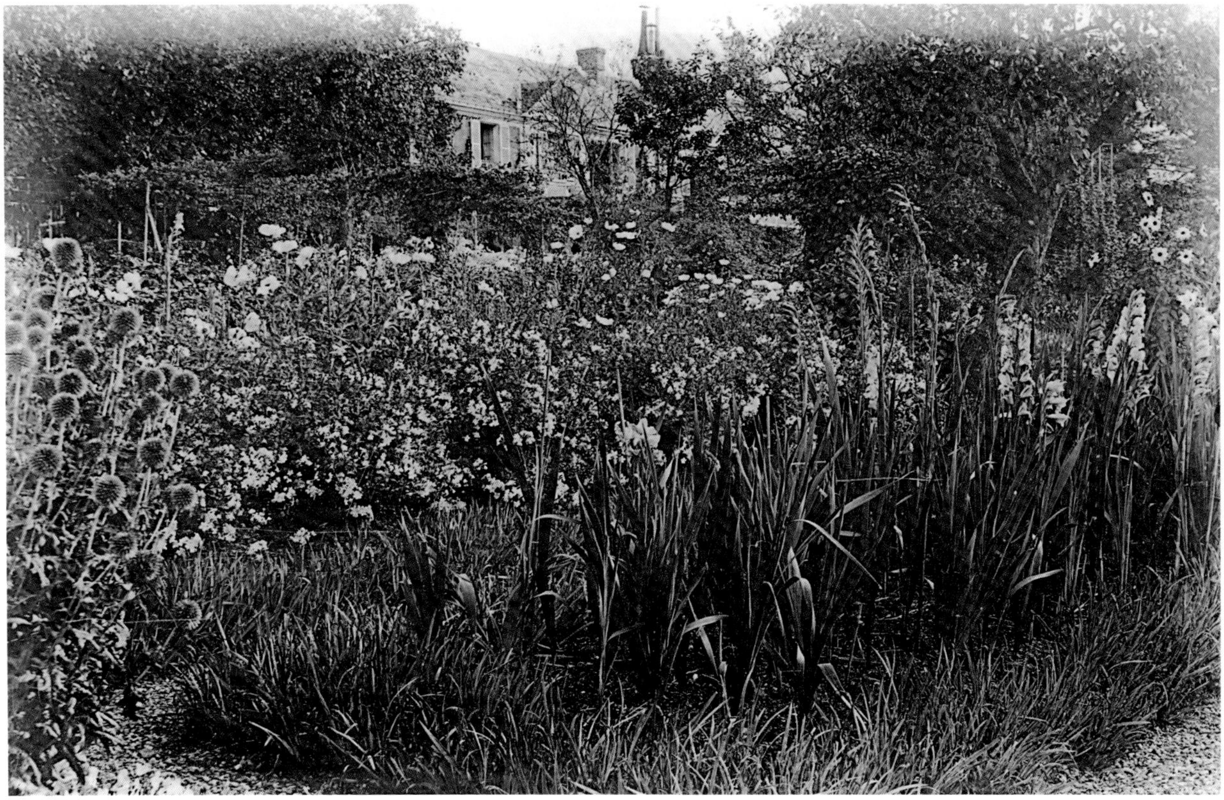

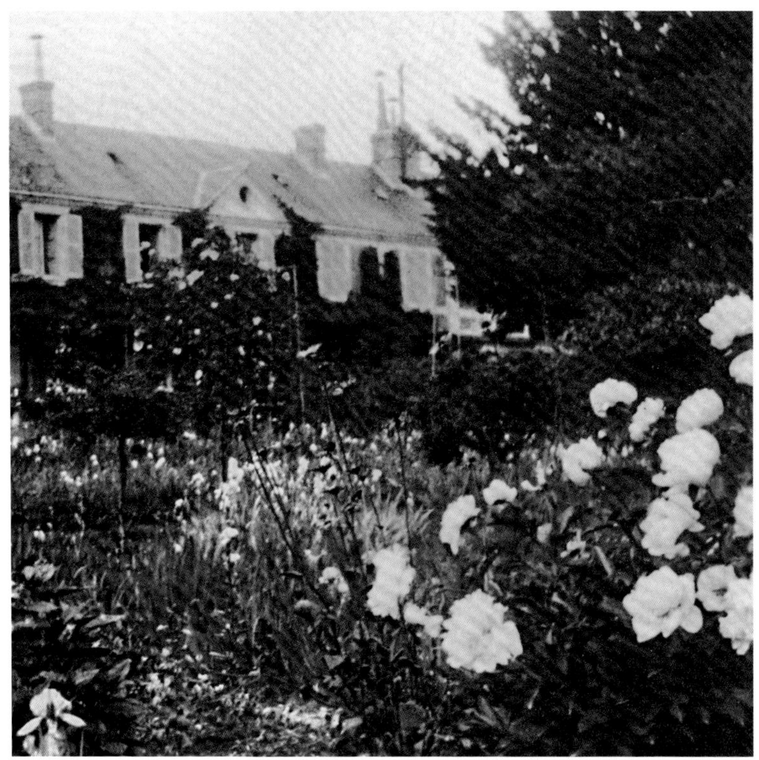

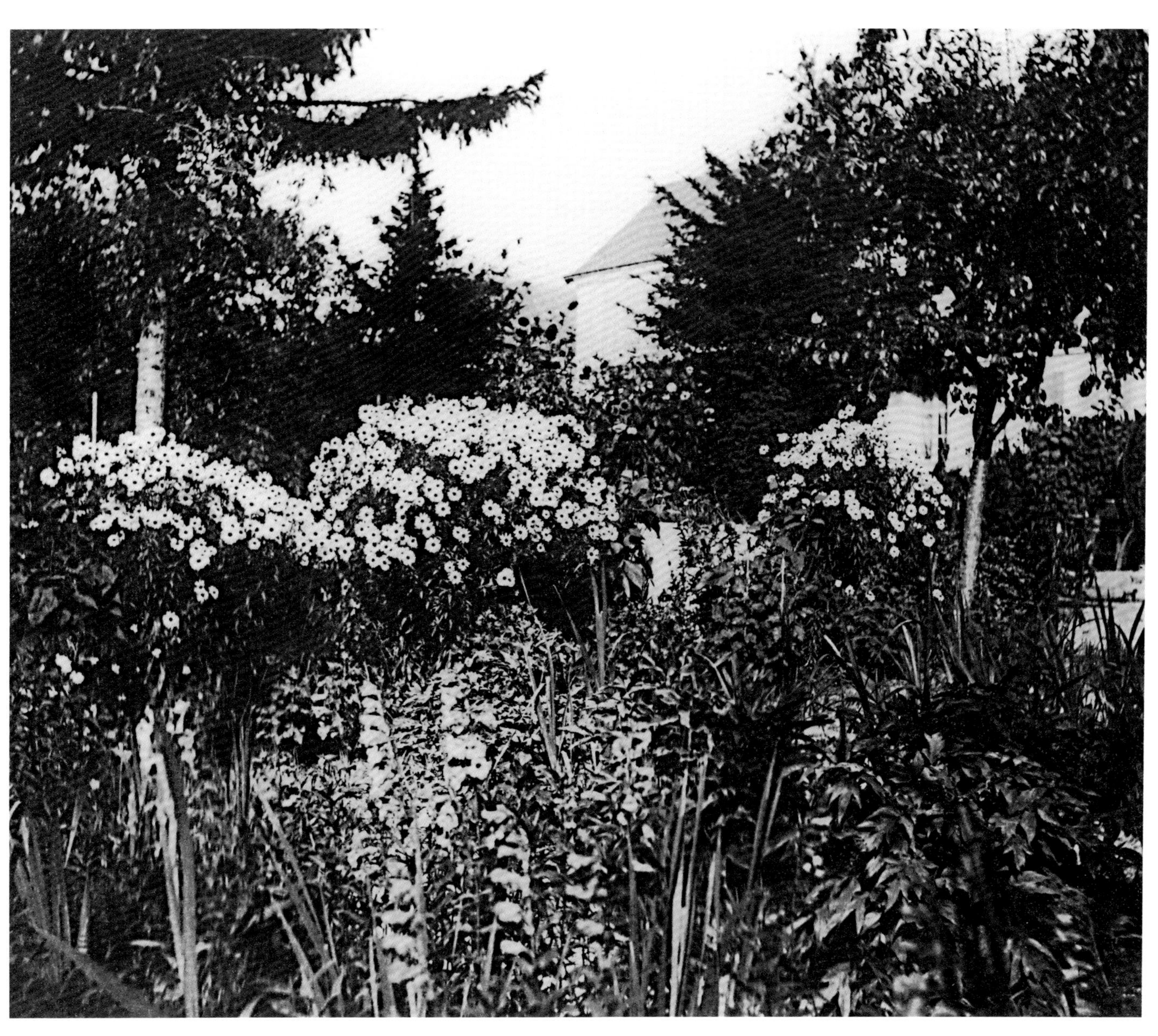

soil, trimming, weeding, and preparing the earth. As Monet's principal sites for painting during the 1880s were away from Giverny, the garden became a priority chiefly during the warmer seasons. In a letter to his painting dealer Paul Durand-Ruel dated June 5, 1883, Monet mentioned the hours that he had to spend away from his brushes in order to tend to his gardening, and his need for a store of flowers to paint in times of bad weather. His more ambitious visions for the garden, clearly, lay in the future.

By the late 1880s, Monet came to enjoy great success, both artistically and financially. His economic savvy served him well. He was upright in his dealings, but business came first. He pitted one dealer against another, and at one time had as many as five eager to exhibit and handle his paintings. Higher prices, a greater number of sales, frequent strategically scheduled and publicized exhibitions, and a reputation that spanned the Atlantic meant that Monet could reap the benefits that accompanied his increased fame.

In November 1890, he bought the Giverny house and land that he had been renting since 1883. He could now feel comfortable developing the property and spending the significant sums necessary to create a lavish flower garden. He hired two full-time gardeners. Their number would grow to six, with Félix Breuil, a renowned head gardener recommended by Monet's close friend Octave Mirbeau, assigned to take charge. Monet and Breuil would walk through the garden together several times a day. In 1892, near the grove of linden trees, Monet built a large greenhouse, devoted chiefly to bulbs and the propagation of species, and several smaller structures. To free the property for the cultivation of flowers, he purchased another property, at the opposite end of the village, which had a large garden. He moved the vegetable garden there, and hired a couple to keep the Monet household supplied with fresh fruit and vegetables.

In 1900, Wynford Dewhurst made this observation: "Monet is, perhaps, seen at his best, and certainly in his most genial mood, when, cigar in full blast, he strolls around his 'propriété' at Giverny, discussing the mysteries of propagation, grafts and colour schemes, with his small army of blue-bloused, sabotted gardeners."

Watering the garden required the services of several apprentices, who would fill their watering cans from a trough near the kitchen, where an ingenious engineering device consisting of a large wheel, two pipes, and several rubber disks attached to a length of chain brought the water to the surface. The gardeners had to sprinkle the entire property by hand, however. By 1908, Monet introduced an irrigation system with a complex and extensive series of pipes that made the watering far less cumbersome.

The heating system for the greenhouse was a small unit, mostly underground, fitted with a coal burner that could be regulated, which heated water running through pipes on all sides of the structure. Monet's neighbor for several years, Lilla Cabot Perry, recounted this story in her article "Reminiscences of Claude Monet from 1889 to 1909":

> *One autumn we were at Giverny I remember there was much interest in a new greenhouse. The heating must have been on a new plan, for when the plants were all in place and the heater first lit, Monet decided he must watch it throughout the night, to be sure everything went smoothly. Once his mind was made up there was little hope of moving him, so Madame Monet speedily acquiesced, and made her own plans for sharing his vigil. When the daughters heard of this there were loud*

outcries. What! Let their parents sit up all night with no one to look after them? Unheard of neglect! It ended by the entire family spending the night with the gloxinias. Fortunately, the heater was impeccably efficient so the adventure did not have to be repeated.

There was even an aviary for many years, watched over by one of Monet's stepdaughters, near the large greenhouse. For Monet it was an added attraction to his house and the life of his family. Over the years the aviary housed long-tailed Australian parakeets nesting in tree trunks, southern partridges from Dordogne, varieties of colored doves, a Java sparrow, and several birds that Monet's friends had offered the family as gifts. Closer to the kitchen were fowl quarters with four or five species of chickens, ducks, and peacocks. Occasionally the odd heron or seagull would wander about the grounds. Although pleased with the improvements he had made to the flower garden, Monet grew frustrated with the limitations imposed by the walls surrounding his property, and he cast his eyes across the road, where there was a marsh with a small pond. The land was not easily accessible, though: the major street of the village had to be crossed, and a railroad track on which a few locomotives would pass each day presented another obstacle. The pond had an ample supply of water, as the marsh was fed by an artificial stream, the Ru, created by medieval monks for irrigating the fields and breeding fish. Monet saw the potential for making a water garden in the marsh. With the acquisition of this parcel of uncultivated land, and with substantial expenditures, the land might offer a wealth of landscaping possibilities.

Monet bought part of this land on February 5, 1893, from a Madame Amat. But the inhabitants of Giverny, who were averse to change, sought to block or at least delay any work on the land. Local opposition centered on three issues: the danger presented by Monet's plan to cultivate exotic water plants previously unknown in the region, which residents feared might harm their livestock; the excavations and the new embankments that would be created; and the necessary interference with the flow of the stream.

Official permission was required for Monet's proposed work, and governmental delays were a fact of life. Monet had time for none of this. He was anxious to return to Rouen to continue the series of paintings of the cathedral that he had begun the year before. An entire year might be lost if the pond was not dug properly, if the devices to control the water were not installed and tested, and if his costly plantings were put on hold.

Monet's letter of March 17, 1893, to the Préfet de l'Eure was quite reasoned and straightforward in requesting the necessary permission. He sought the right to excavate the pond, install a sluice that would control the level and flow of the water nourishing the garden, and construct two light wooden footbridges.

Having learned that the local opposition was more adamant than he had expected, Monet expressed an uncharacteristic fury in a letter to his wife, written on March 20 from Rouen. He wanted to halt the work in progress, he said, rid himself of the engineers and workmen, and abandon the entire project. "Rent nothing, order no wire lattice and throw the aquatic plants in the stream; they will grow there. . . . Shit for the natives of Giverny, the engineers. I give the land to whoever wants it."

Monet quieted down and returned to painting the cathedral. He further profited from his stay in Rouen by visiting Monsieur Varenne, the director of the Jardin des Plantes there, who graciously showed the painter around his greenhouses. Monet set about

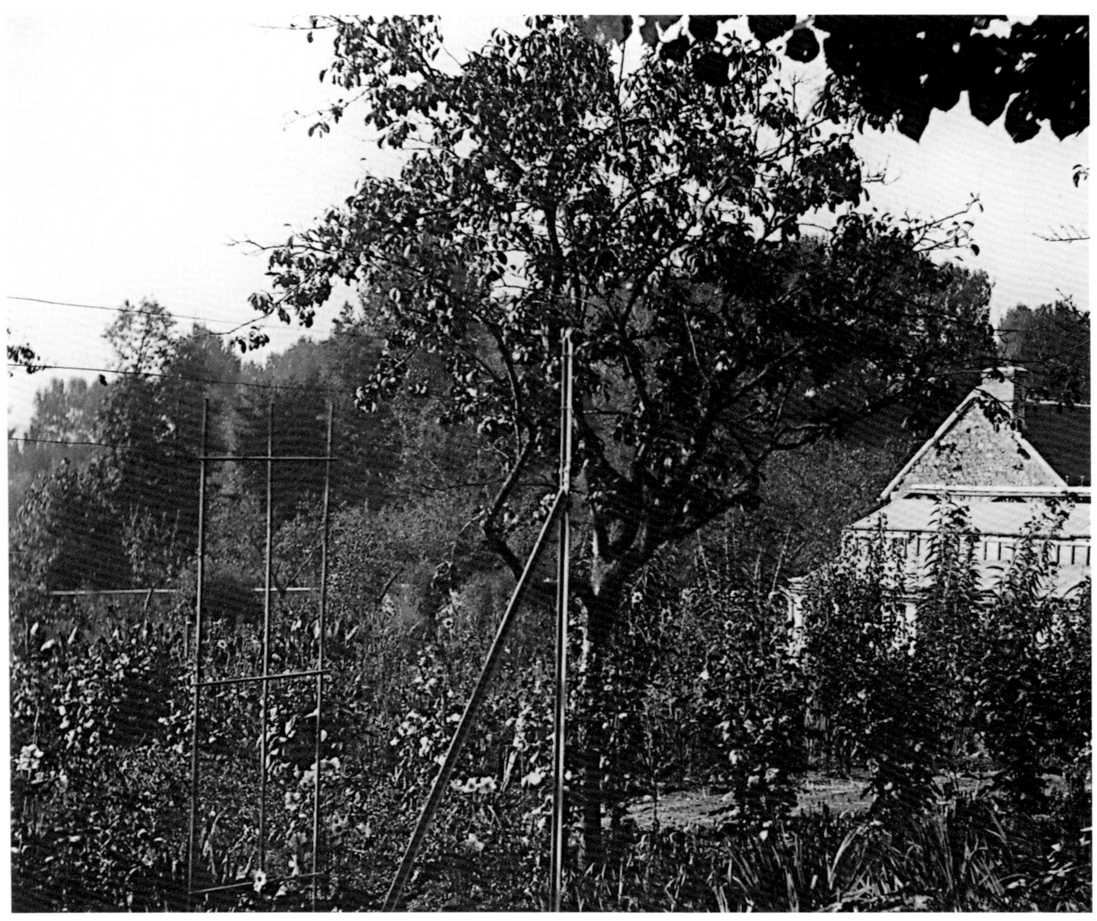

choosing plants from nurseries in Rouen, and garnering information from local horticulturists about the proper cultivation of these plants in the soil and climate of Normandy.

On his return to Giverny in April, he geared up for the fight over the realization of his water garden. The first paragraphs of his letter of July 17 to the Préfet de l'Eure mixed kind remarks with a barrage of condemnations of the local residents, assailing their selfish and petty reasons for opposing his plans. The following two paragraphs were gentler:

> *I would also like you to know that the said cultivation of aquatic plants does not have the importance implied by the word and that it has only to do with something agreeable and for the pleasure of the eyes, and also for the purpose of having motifs to paint; and finally I will grow in this pond only such plants as water lilies, reeds, and different varieties of irises that generally grow wild along our stream, and that there can be no question of poisoning the water.*
>
> *I will promise nevertheless, should the peasants continue to disbelieve, to renew the water of the said pond only during the hours of the night when no one uses water.*

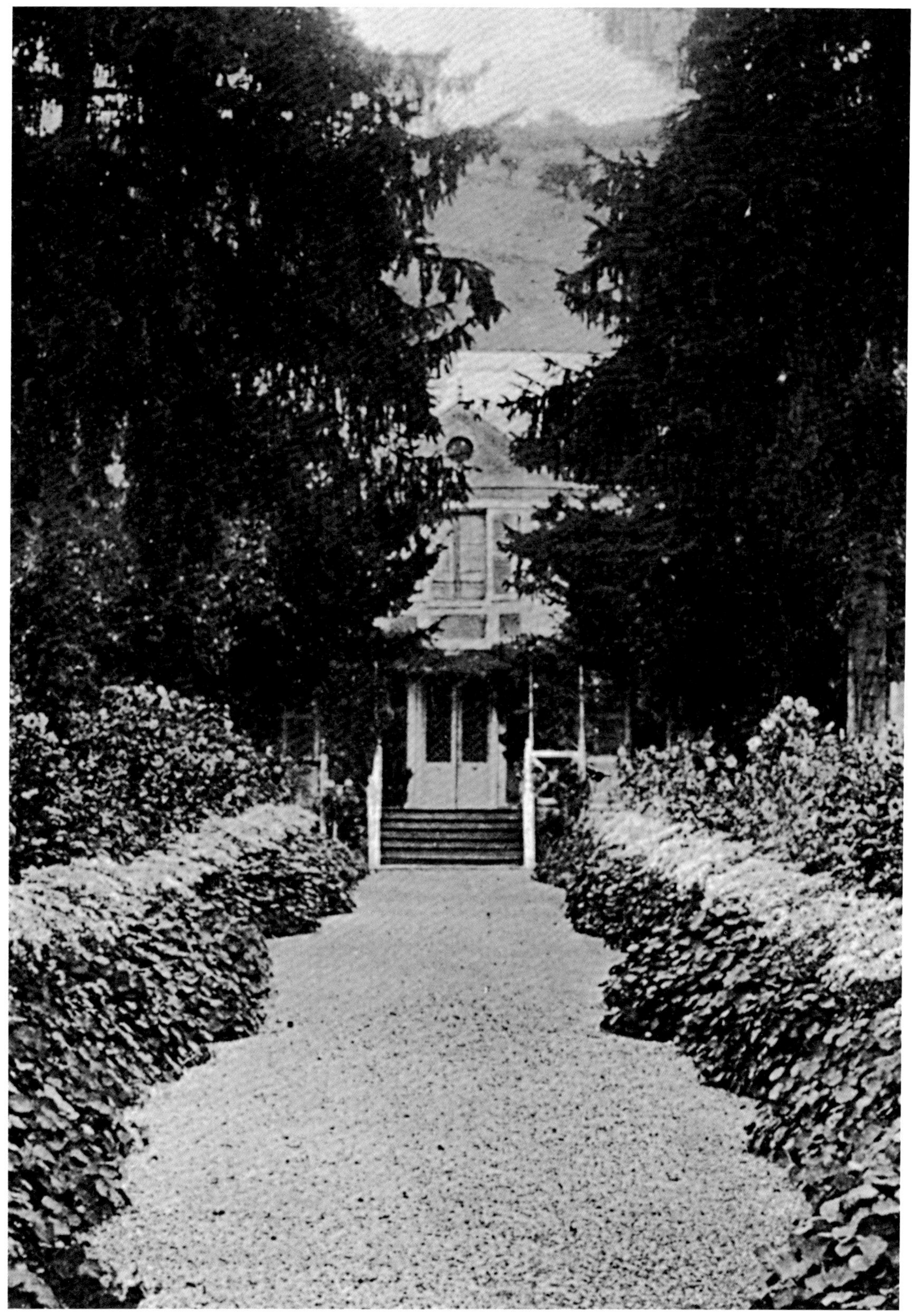

By July 28, Monet had received authorization to install a sluice on a branch of the Ru, also known as the *bras communal*, and to construct two footbridges over this branch opposite his home. A photograph by Lilla Cabot Perry and three paintings by Monet from 1895 indicate that by this date the Japanese bridge had been built, most likely by a local carpenter under Monet's supervision, and that the water garden had been planted with flowers on the banks of the pond, but with no trace of water lilies.

On the other side of the road, the flower garden was flourishing under the supervision of Félix Breuil, his team, and Monet's watchful eye. Monet's second studio, adjacent to the greenhouses, was completed in August 1899, with a great deal of space devoted solely to the maintenance of the flower garden. There was a room reserved for bulbs—especially the quantities of tulips that played a major role in the floral ensemble—which were placed in boxes meticulously labeled and stacked. The outside of the house was adorned with roses and Virginia creeper, which would eventually cover it. The exterior of the new studio had some Virginia creeper, too, and the heating plant was covered with passionflower.

Over the years, several visitors, including Monet's friends, horticulturists, journalists, and writers wishing to publish books on the celebrated painter, wrote bountiful descriptions of the garden. Arsène Alexandre gave this account in "Le Jardin de Monet" from *Le Figaro* of August 9, 1901:

> *In the garden of Monet there are uninterrupted flowers. Whichever way you turn, at your feet, above your head, at the level of your chest, are lakes, garlands, hedges of flowers, whose harmonies are both improvised and calculated, and are renewed according to the seasons. . . . You may obtain marvelous results provided that you know how to play on the floral calendar as on a keyboard and are a great colorist. It is this profusion, this crowded appearance that produces the whole character. . . .*
>
> *He also wants, above all, for his palette of flowers to be before his eyes at all times, constantly present, but constantly changing. Everything is arranged so that the feast is everywhere renewed and follows along without interruption.*

Monet and his colleagues would often write to one another inquiring about specific varieties of plants and how to procure certain seedlings, and would share information and flowers that they had obtained. A letter to Monet from Octave Mirbeau relates poetically their shared passion for gardening:

> *I am very happy that you will be bringing Caillebotte. We will talk about gardening, as you say, because as for art and literature, it is all humbug. There is nothing but the earth. As for me, I now find a clump of soil admirable and I spend whole hours contemplating it. And compost! I love compost the way one loves a woman. I smear it on myself and in the fuming heaps I see the beautiful forms and the beautiful colors that will be born from it! How little art is next to it!*

Monet took pleasure inviting friends to Giverny for lunch and afterward to tour his garden. Few outsiders were extended this invitation, which might disrupt his daily ritual of painting; he was by no means a hermit, but rather, very selective. It was considered inappropriate to disturb the master of the house, and all the gardeners had to go through Félix Breuil. Monet was not unfriendly, just formal. In a letter of May 29, 1900, to Georges Clemenceau, whom he had known as a student in Paris and with whom he had remained in contact throughout the permutations of this wily journalist-politician's career, Monet's enthusiasm is apparent:

> *I am still awaiting your long-promised visit. Now is the time, you will see the garden in all its splendor, but you must hurry. Would you like to come either on Sunday or on Monday? Any later and all the blossoms will have withered. Make arrangements with Geffroy and write me. I am counting on you. In addition [I have] piles of new paintings. In complete friendship, Shake Geffroy and come.*

The singular quality of the Giverny flower garden was starting to be recognized in both artistic and gardening circles worldwide, and Maurice Kahn's article "Le Jardin de Claude Monet" in *Le Temps* on June 7, 1904, only contributed to its glory. Kahn quoted Monet as stating that "outside of painting and gardening . . . I am good for nothing." The journalist added: "After having seen Claude Monet in his garden, one may better understand that a gardener of this quality would also be a painter of this quality. This prodigious man is a fervent admirer of life. And when he paints, it is a means for him to create living beauty."

The art dealer René Gimpel came to Giverny on August 19, 1918, and made this notation about the flower garden in his diary:

> I*t resembles no other, first because it consists of only the simplest flowers and then because they grow to unheard-of heights. I believe that none is under three feet high. Certain flowers, some of which are white and others yellow, resembling huge daisies, shoot up to six feet. It's not a meadow, but a virgin forest of flowers whose colors are very pure, neither pink nor bluish, but red or blue.*

By 1898, Monet had transformed the water garden and its surroundings into an enchanting domain composed of water lilies quietly floating on the surface of the pond, the existing trees on the site, and several species of plants that thrive on the banks of streams. The arc of the Japanese bridge and its reflection quietly fused the diverse elements into an ensemble. In contrast to the flower garden across the road, the layout of the water-lily garden was organic.

Although Monet had originally considered the water-lily pond as simply a pleasurable extension of his garden, its beauty would become an important motif for his paintings. In 1900 he exhibited two series of paintings of the water garden at the Galérie Durand-Ruel in Paris. The paintings of 1899 show the bridge and its surroundings from an almost direct angle that Monet would subtly change to create variety, while those from 1900 show a greater number of plants on the perimeter of the pond, and are much more colorful, even fairylike.

Monet quickly felt constrained by the physical limitations of the water garden. It was too narrow and short, and the fact that it was hemmed in between two properties and a railroad track disturbed him. He wanted a terrain sufficiently large for an expanded pond and the ability to fashion elegant, sweeping paths throughout the property. In May 1901, he purchased an additional terrain of 3,920 square meters, adjacent to the water garden, thus tripling the space available for development. He exchanged property with the local railroad company to enable a reconfiguration of access to the pond and to render the space more private.

Once again he had to seek administrative approval; this time he appealed to the Giverny municipal council as well as the Préfet de l'Eure. Both his letters were launched in August, and the first response came from the local authorities. They had met in a special session and decided that Monet could start the excavation work, but they gave precise indications for the width and depth of the new branch of the stream, and specified the exact nature of the sluices that could be employed. The council also reserved the right to revoke the permission should the new aquatic plants prove to be of any public danger. Monet, unhappy with the sluices as described in the authorization, appealed to the Préfet, and later in the year he obtained a ruling that set aside the decision of the Giverny officials and granted him the means of controlling the flow of water into the pond that he had requested.

Monet was now in a position to begin planting the garden he desired.The expanded pond offered him the chance to introduce an infinite array of water lilies, while the extended banks would eventually be covered with several varieties of flowers, trees—particularly weeping willows—arches, and arbors; only the Japanese bridge remained from the original garden, and even there, wisteria, white and mauve, flowered in the early summer. The placement of the bridge was crucial for Monet, as, constructed on the same axis as the central alley of the house, it unified the two separate gardens.

After art critics lamented the dispersal of his "series" paintings around the world, Monet began to conceive of a series that would by its very nature form a continuous ensemble. Given his love for the water garden, it was only natural that he would focus on this subject for the ensemble. Despite the brilliant reception of the Japanese bridge paintings, Monet realized that they were, nonetheless, individual canvases.

Monet recognized the challenge of creating a series of paintings that could be linked together in a manner that he had never before attempted. He firmly believed that the range of motifs afforded by the expansion of the pond would lead him to the floral arrangements that would lock into the unified panels he sought. His ultimate objective was to achieve the ideal balance between a purely decorative ensemble and a great work of art.

Monet himself offered an insight into this project to the journalist Maurice Guillemot in August 1897: "Imagine a circular room where the wall below the molding would be entirely occupied by a horizon of water spotted with vegetation, the walls alternating between a transparent green and mauve, the calm and quiet of the still water reflecting the flowering expanses, the tones vague, delightfully subtle, and with a dream-like delicacy." Guillemot's article was the first published expression of Monet's dream to re-create on canvas the impressions of his water-lily pond. It revealed just how inseparable gardening and painting were in the artist's mind.

Monet had to wait several years for the new garden to flourish. During this period he was actively planning, planting, painting, and, at times, traveling. His winters were spent in London, where he painted one series of the city's bridges, and another of the Houses of Parliament. Financial success allowed him to enjoy many novel luxuries—material comforts, as well as more time with his family. Early on he acquired a first-class automobile, a Panhard. He never drove, but employed a chauffeur so that his family could attend local automobile rallies, picnic, visit the seaside, and travel through the Loire Valley. He rented a house in a village near Giverny that was accessible by automobile, and here he would paint while the family leisurely entertained themselves. In October 1904, Monet, Alice, and his son Michel traveled by automobile to Spain.

Monet once declared, "What I need most of all are flowers, always, always," but it would not be inaccurate to alter this to: "What I need most of all is color, always, always." Gifted as he was with a color sensibility that permitted him to paint day after day in the most varied light conditions, and to capture the color effects of his chosen sites with lightning speed, it would have been natural for Monet the painter and Monet the gardener to research and select species of water lilies that would enrich the tonal range of his palette.

His horticultural knowledge from years of gardening was vast, as was his library of magazines (notably the *Revue horticole*), catalogues from around the world, books, and encyclopedias. Monet could count on several friends who were equally passionate about gardening, in addition to his relationship with the gardening firms of Georges Truffaut and Vilmorin-Andrieux. Monet found his most important source of water-lily species by attending the Exposition Universelle in Paris in 1889 and in 1900, and by familiarizing himself with the wealth of hybrid water lilies being cultivated by Joseph Bory Latour-Marliac in Temple-sur-Lot, near Bordeaux.

As early as 1877, Latour-Marliac had produced his first hybrid; in the 1880s he achieved a stream of production, and in 1889 he formally introduced these species to the world at the Exposition Universelle. Several other varieties appeared in the 1890s, and he experimented with hybridization until his death in 1911, when he took his secrets with him. Although we have no record of Monet's having corresponded with Latour-Marliac—unfortunately, the archives of the Marliac company were destroyed in a flood in 1910—Monet could have readily procured Latour-Marliac's creations through Vilmorin.

By a strange coincidence, Monet and Latour-Marliac appeared at the same time, and in separate but not mutually exclusive fields sought the same thing: color. By 1902, Latour-Marliac had produced thirty-two varieties, combining hardy water lilies from the northern hemisphere known for the duration of their flowering with hardy colorful species from temperate climates. His dream was to succeed in a similar fashion with exotic varieties from the tropics; today we know that this is genetically impossible. Still, he obtained color, which was of equal importance to Monet for the surface of the pond, color that spread in luxurious symmetrical patterns, offering him each day an ever-changing spectrum from which he could draw inspiration.

As Monet's paintings were meant to be an evocation of the pond, a lyrical poem drawn from his majestic tapestry of colors, they may be read as an homage to Latour-Marliac's genius as a botanist. Monet purchased a number of Latour-Marliac's water lilies. But we know from contemporary accounts that in certain years Monet and his gardeners succeeded in growing pure tropical and exotic species, and that he had many kinds with pink flowers; an Egyptian white with pink petals on the outside; the *Nymphaea aurora*, which began as yellow and reddened with age; and one or two blue varieties from South America.

By 1903, Monet had embarked on a series of paintings representing the recently enlarged water-lily garden. Forty-eight were shown at the Galérie Durand-Ruel in 1909 under the title *Les Nymphéas, séries de paysages d'eau*. The paintings received great critical acclaim, although Edgar Degas was known to have rushed out of the exhibition claiming that he was suffering from vertigo. The show triggered a debate: Were these paintings depictions of an actual garden, or a wondrous abstraction of impressions that when seen together rendered an illusion that

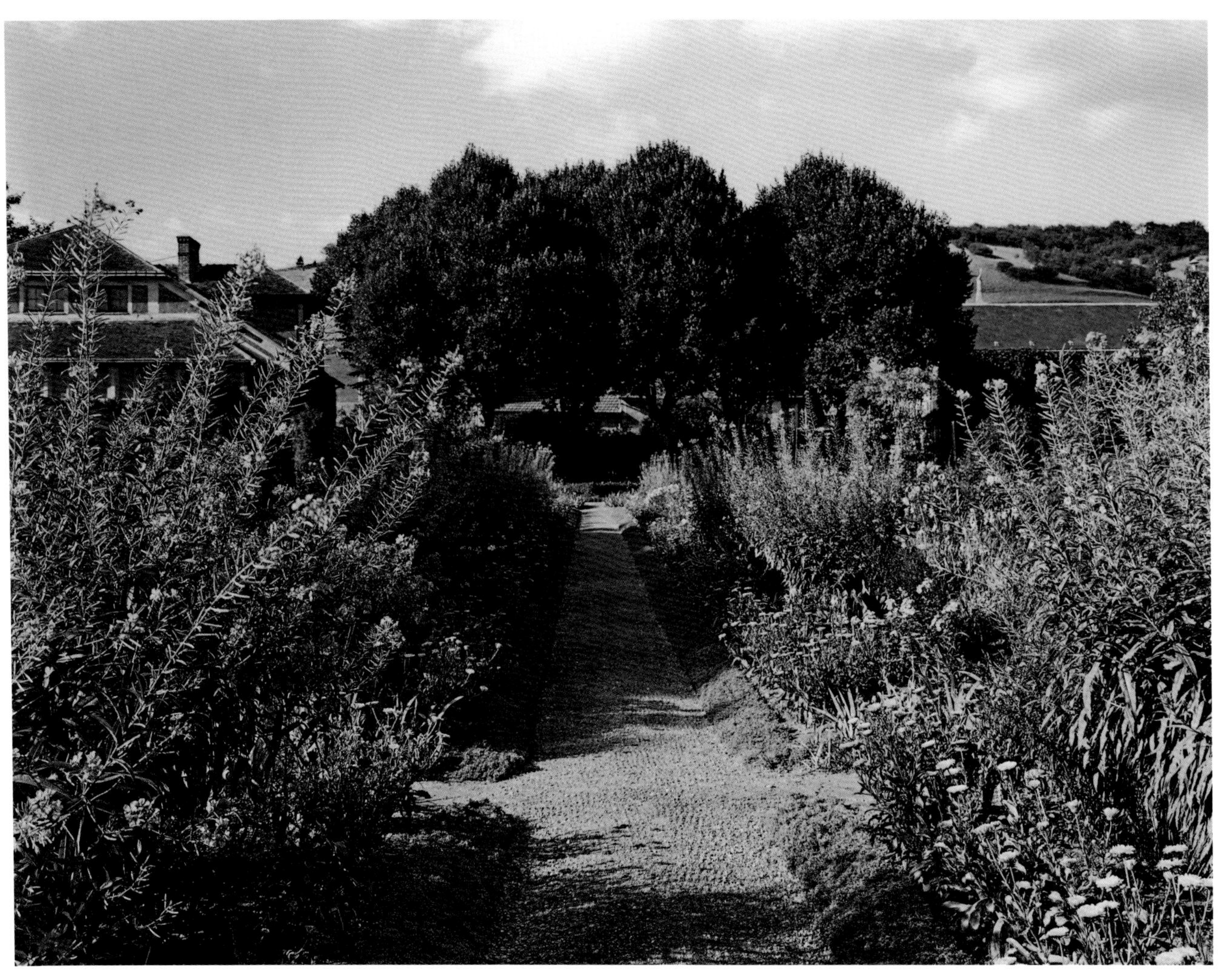

only Monet, the founder of Impressionism, could achieve?

Arsène Alexandre summarized this question in *Le Figaro* of May 7, 1909:

> *Here then, insofar as it can be explained by words, is the essence of these water landscapes. M. Claude Monet has painted the surface of the pond in a Japanese garden where water lilies bloom; but he painted only this surface, seen in perspective, and no horizon is given to these paintings, which have no beginning or end other than the limits of the frame, but which the imagination easily extends as far as it likes. Therefore, as elements of the painting, we have only the aquatic mirror and the leaves and flowers that rest upon it,—then the reflection, dappled and infinitely varied, of the surrounding landscape, and of the sky above us. They are, in a word, paintings of reflections mingled with real objects, but which harmonize with them in a marvelous and capricious diversity.*

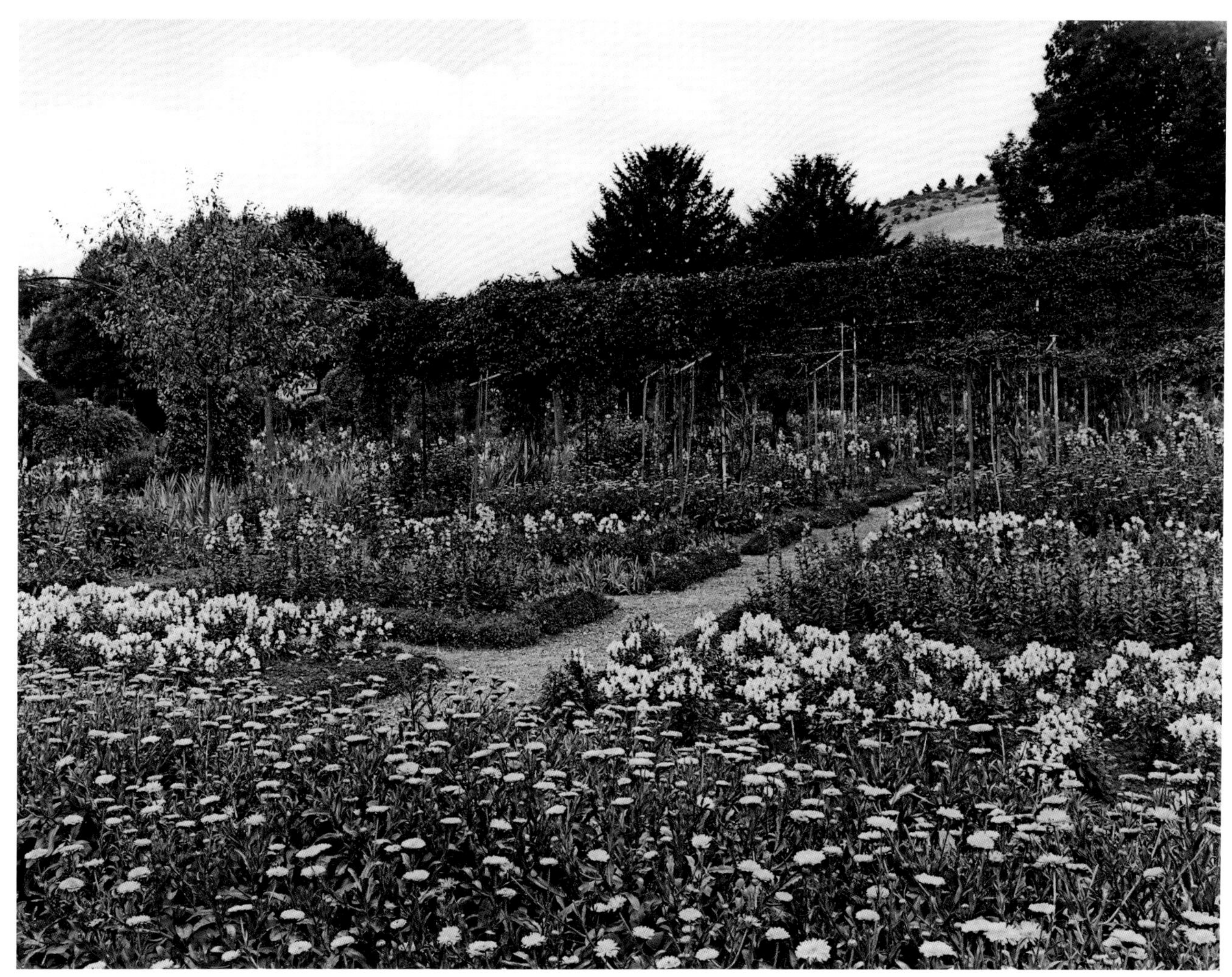

Marc Elder quoted the painter in his book *À Giverny, chez Claude Monet:*

> *"It took me some time to understand my water lilies," said Claude Monet. "I had planted them for pleasure; I cultivated them without dreaming of painting them. . . . A landscape does not percolate through your mind in a day. . . . And then, suddenly I had the revelation of the fairy-land of my pond. I took my palette. . . . Since that time I have hardly had another model."*

In an interview in the June 1909 *Gazette des Beaux-Arts,* the art critic Roger Marx quoted Monet describing an anticipated series of water-lily paintings that resembled the project the artist had described to Guillemot in 1897:

> *"At a certain time I became tempted to employ this water lily theme for the decoration of a drawing room: carried along the walls, enveloping all the partitions with its unity, it would have produced the illusion of an endless*

whole, of a wave without horizon and without shore; nerves exhausted by work would have relaxed there, following the restful example of those still waters, and to whoever would have lived in it, this room would have offered a refuge of peaceful meditation in the middle of a flowering aquarium."

Monet had thus conceptually defined how the new series of paintings of his water-lily pond would transport viewers to his private world. He devoted the rest of his life to enhancing the beauty of his garden, painting it, and working toward the realization of this dream.

A special gardener was assigned to the care of the pond. Dredging was essential to prevent the buildup of sediment, a regulated water temperature was critical for the proper cultivation of the water lilies, as were constant *direct* care and *direct* pruning. Every day the aphids that might harm the leaves and, even more, the blossoms were removed, providing nourishment for the pond's fish.

Monet was obsessed with the removal of any traces of dust from his motif, the water lilies. In the morning the gardener had to bathe each bud to eliminate any sign of dust when the flowers opened in the midday sun. A visitor to the water garden described this daily routine, explaining that when the gardener had completed this work, "the owner of the property would then settle in, and with unique artistic passion, begin painting with fury the site that he had planned with patience."

When the automobile became increasingly popular and affordable, the dust that was kicked up on the formerly peaceful road running between his two gardens unnerved Monet. The only solution was to pave the two main streets of Giverny with asphalt. He offered to pay almost half the expense, won the approval of the municipal council, and saw to it that the work began on schedule on June 10, 1907.

Both gardens were a source of joy for the entire family. During his wife Alice's lifetime, a table was set for refreshments, where tea or a glass of wine, port, or sherry would be served with cookies. When visitors came for lunch, it would be served in the two-toned yellow dining room, and weather permitting, the large windows would be opened to give an unhindered view of the flower garden. After lunch, there was the traditional walk through the gardens, which was considered by his guests a remarkable privilege. It was a natural world of beauty and life.

The several species of bamboo in the water garden came either from Latour-Marliac, who was a specialist in their cultivation, or from a relative in the French colonial service in Saigon. Monet took particular interest in the "real" bamboo, characterized by large, heavy knots; a dwarf bamboo, a very hardy, small woody plant with blackish-green leaves and whitish cream-colored borders; and a long, smooth variety with small knots, which would serve as plant props in the garden. Clouds of sparrows and starlings would cluster and sing in the thickets, and in fall and winter, the bamboo offered them refuge.

The cost of the gardens, the plantings, and the maintenance was considerable; but for Monet, who would lounge by the side of the pond in search of painting motifs, or merely to enjoy this most beautiful creation, the cost was of little consequence. What did disturb him was any event that came between him and his work. When the gardens were inundated during the flood of February 1910, a letter to his painting dealer Paul Durand-Ruel expressed his concern. Monet even feared that the entire garden might be lost, but then later realized that despite the damage, the situation could have been more severe. A greater catastrophy occurred in August 1912, when the property was struck by a cyclone, which ravaged the gardens, laying waste especially Monet's beloved weeping willows. This devastation was a veritable calamity, as the willows—especially the most majestic one, which was broken into pieces—were the central elements reflecting on the surface of the water, as well as the focal point for his water-lily decorations. Monet was fortunate that his gardeners were able to prop up all the weeping willows to their original positions, and in time, with their professional care, the trees healed.

Between 1914 and 1916, Monet built an enormous third studio, reserved for painting and for storing larger canvases of the pond. In the warmer months he would set up his easel alongside the pond and make studies of the plants growing on the banks. These late works reveal his total mastery of painting, and the relative abandon that great masters experience in their later years. These paintings were not abstract, but lush, rich portraits of the flowers he so carefully nurtured. They were the culmination of a life of looking, blended with a desire to work on a much vaster scale. Monet was now painting entirely for himself, with no exhibitions or sales in mind, and he refused to part with these compositions. They remained in his studio at his death in 1926, virtually unknown to the outside world.

The colder months, when working outdoors was difficult for the hardy but aged painter, were reserved for the decorative panels, for which Monet had no predetermined installation site. The paintings—diptychs, triptychs, and quadriptychs—were composed of canvases each some fourteen feet in length. When a painting dealer expressed the wish to purchase just one of these panels, Monet responded, "Impossible . . . Each one evokes the others for me."

By 1920, Monet had determined the four themes for the panels—morning, green reflections, clouds, and trees. He selected the ideal location for their permanent exhibition—his own museum in the center of Paris, preferably on the grounds of the Hôtel Biron, which had recently become the Rodin Museum. Monet and Rodin had been closely associated throughout their lives, each was considered the leader in his field, and the gardens at the Hôtel would be an ideal setting for the small, thoughtfully designed museum that Monet had in mind. True to his personality, he hired his own architect to draw up plans for the edifice.

After years of hardship, anguish, and battling every conceivable element of nature, Monet sought a home, a garden, and a more settled life. He achieved all this and left a remarkable legacy. René Gimpel visited the Monet property again in October 1920; he recorded in his diary:

> *We went for a walk in the garden. It's a perfect garden, a panorama of flowers whose beauty is deeply moving; they are so tall on their stems that they seem to walk along with us. Today for the first time Monet took me across the road and the railway line beyond which his garden extends, but where the landscape changes its appearance completely. There is Monet's pond where his water lilies float, surrounded by his pale willows, a pond which he has created as God created the caprices of nature.*

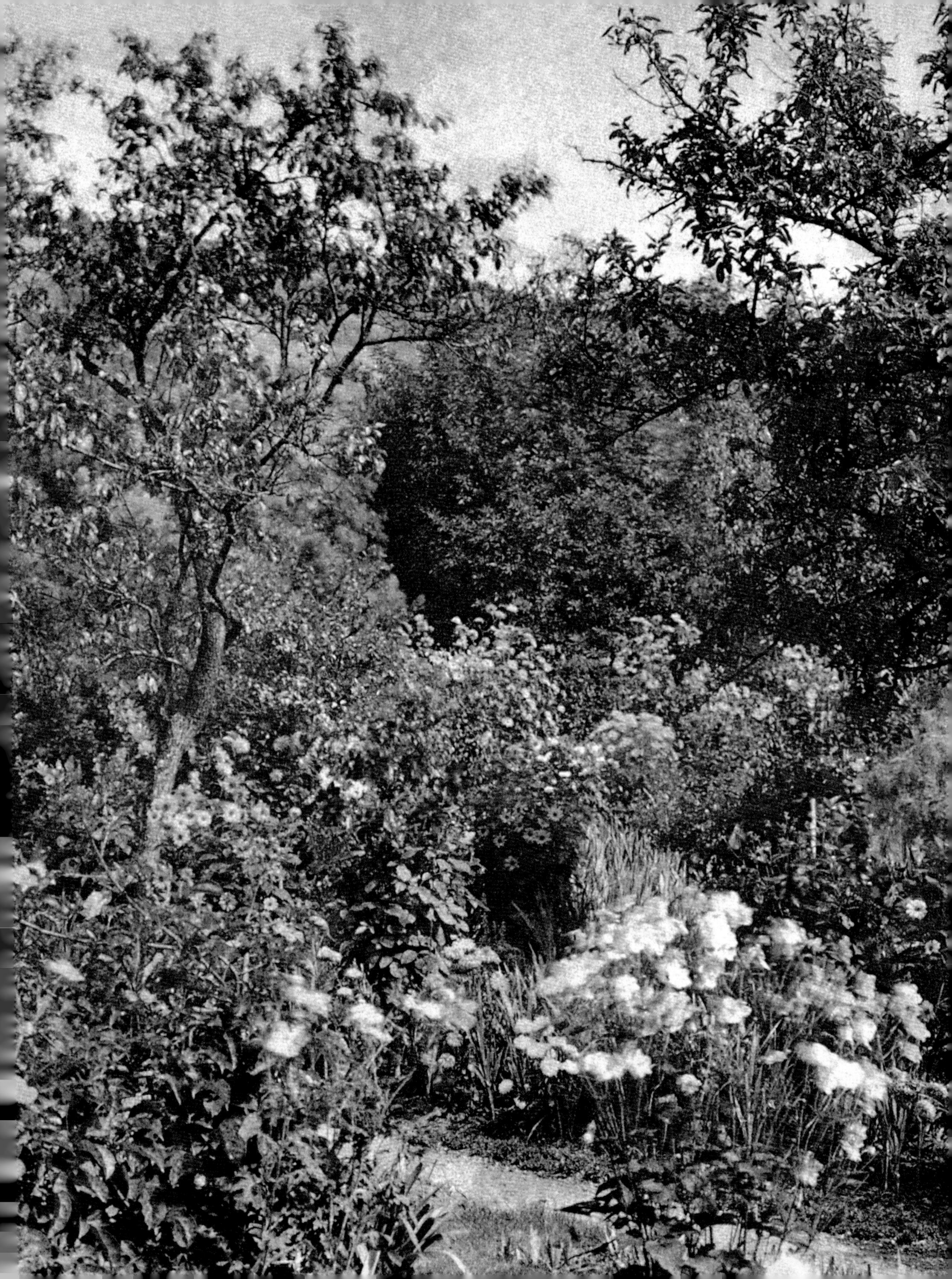

A GARDENING LIFE

Sydney Eddison

> *When you buy a piece of land, remember—you own all above it; you own that far reach of ether in which the stars drift over your land, the moon as it hangs above your trees, the sun as it passes through your sky-claim; and best of all you possess all the dreams which lie between you and infinity.*
>
> —Hanna Rion, 1912

From what source does the gardening instinct spring? In my case, from a childhood passion for the out-of-doors. A telltale longing for the smell and feel of earth remained dormant, however, until my husband and I bought eight country acres and an old farmhouse. Once we had taken possession, I felt a compelling urge to do something to the land. That crude impulse was refined by exposure to an enchanting older couple and their beautiful garden, and honed by forty-two years of practice.

Who knows what forces drove and inspired the Impressionist painter Claude Monet to create the glorious gardens at Giverny? Certainly, an enduring love affair with the natural world. But the only reference he made to early gardening experiences was this cryptic statement: "Gardening was something I learned in my youth when I was unhappy. Perhaps I owe [my] having become a painter to flowers."

Even as a young painter, Monet filled canvas after canvas with flowers. *Women in the Garden*, painted in 1866, when he was still in his twenties, shows Camille, his model and later his wife, burying her face in a bouquet, while the seated figure—for which she also posed—admires the blossoms in her lap. In the background, full-petaled white and red roses stand out against dark foliage and dappled shade. Some of the roses are grown on a single stem—sur tige—a technique Monet would employ in his garden at Giverny. While roses predominate in the scene, the eye is immediately drawn to a lone spike of scarlet gladiolus—the signature flower in dozens of Monet's paintings, and in all of his gardens.

The next year, in *Garden at Sainte-Adresse,* Monet painted family members enjoying the flowers at a sailing club near his Normandy home. Under the blue summer sky, boisterous red geraniums create a lively contrast against green lawn and foliage, just as they will later in his own gardens. And masses of red, orange, and yellow nasturtiums tumble over the terrace pavement, foreshadowing their lusty performance at Giverny. Gladioli send up sword-shaped leaves and spires of red and red-and-yellow

Exploring Normandy six years after Monet's death, the English travel writer Stephen Gwynn sought out the village of Giverny and made a pilgrimage to the painter's garden. Upon returning home, Gwynn described his first impressions in an article for *Country Life* magazine:

"On our left was a low wall topped by a long iron grille, perfectly simple in design; through it one saw a long, low farmhouse, having in front of it a dazzle of flowers." Tended at the time by Monet's daughter-in-law, the garden still overflowed with an abundance of plants that softened the edges of the rectilinear beds and created an effect "as carelessly variegated as a wheat field where poppies and blue corn cockle have scattered themselves."

Indeed, Monet had always welcomed field flowers into the garden and given them free rein. Trees, shrubs, herbaceous perennials, annuals, and wildflowers mingled with reckless abandon in his beds and borders.

Monet planted in bold masses and favored such plants as delphiniums and gladioli, with upright, tapering flower spikes. Improbable as it may seem, aristocratic delphiniums belong to the buttercup family, *Ranunculaceae*. Their terminal flower clusters come in two distinct forms: "garland" types, which have branching stems spangled with blossoms; and the dramatic *Delphinium elatum* hybrids, with their soaring spires of densely packed flowers. The latter were Monet's favorites.

The relationship between the genus *Gladiolus* and the genus *Iris* is easy to see. Both are members of the *Iridaceae* family and have flat, sword-shaped leaves, but their blossoms are very different from each other. While the individual gladiolus flower resembles a lily, the architecture of an iris blossom is unique, consisting of three upright segments, or standards, and three downward-sweeping falls.

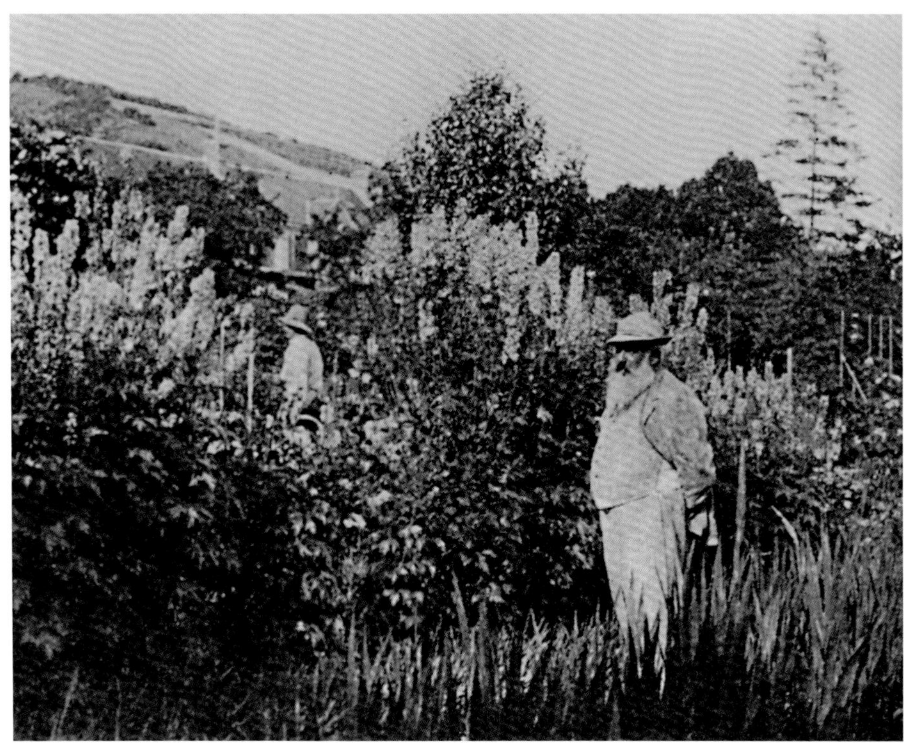

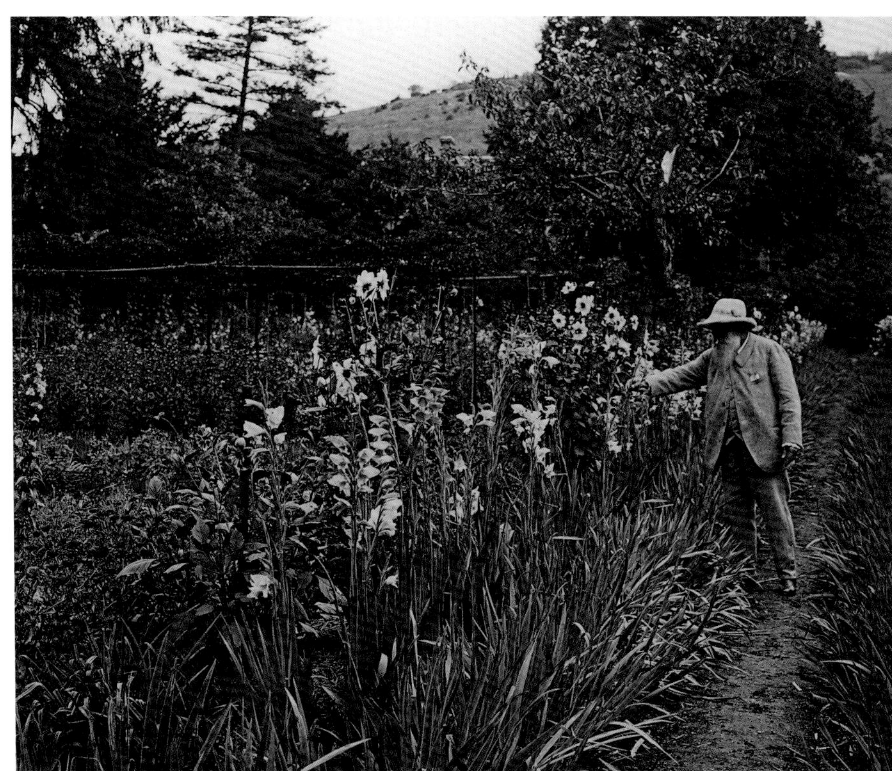

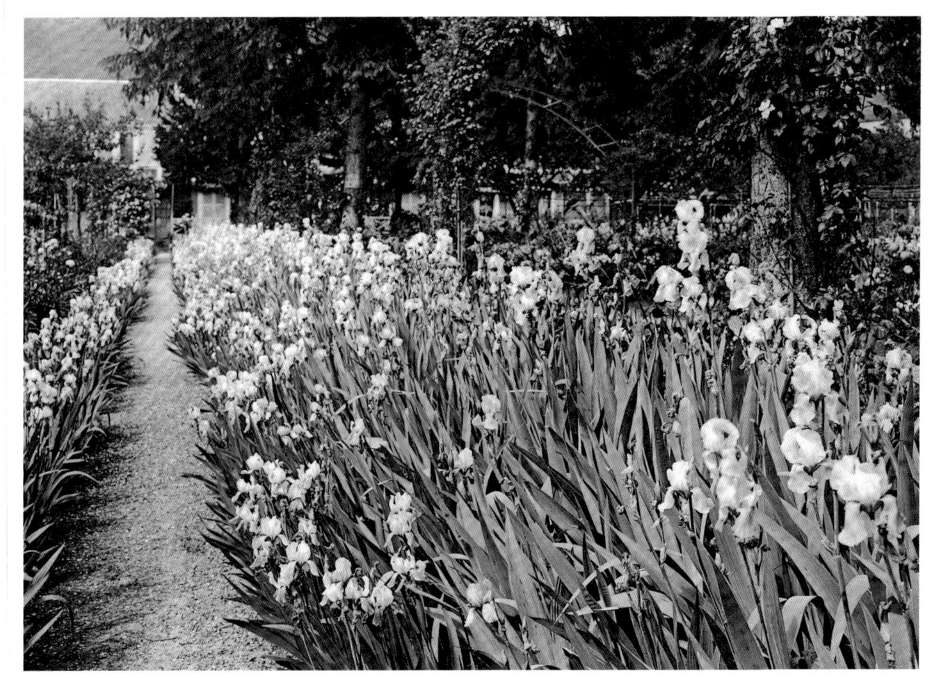

Named for the goddess of the rainbow, the genus *Iris* includes more than two hundred species. Some require dry, sun-baked soil; others demand constant moisture. Monet grew both types. In the flower beds near his house, he planted bearded irises, which have large, elegant blossoms and a characteristic pattern of hairs on the falls. The moisture-loving irises found a suitable home on the banks of the pond in the water garden, where they formed clumps of grassy leaves and slender stems topped with dainty, beardless flowers.

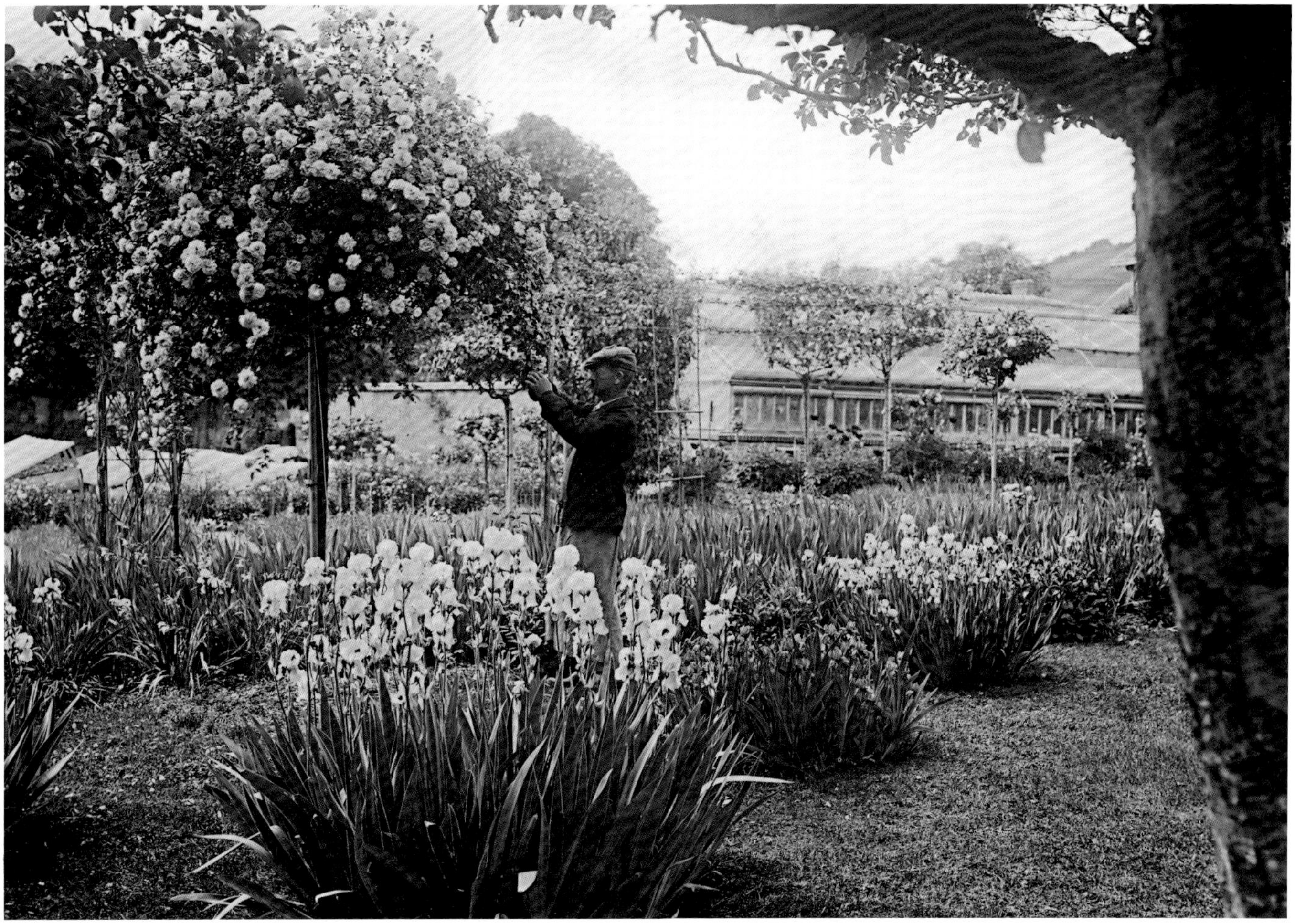

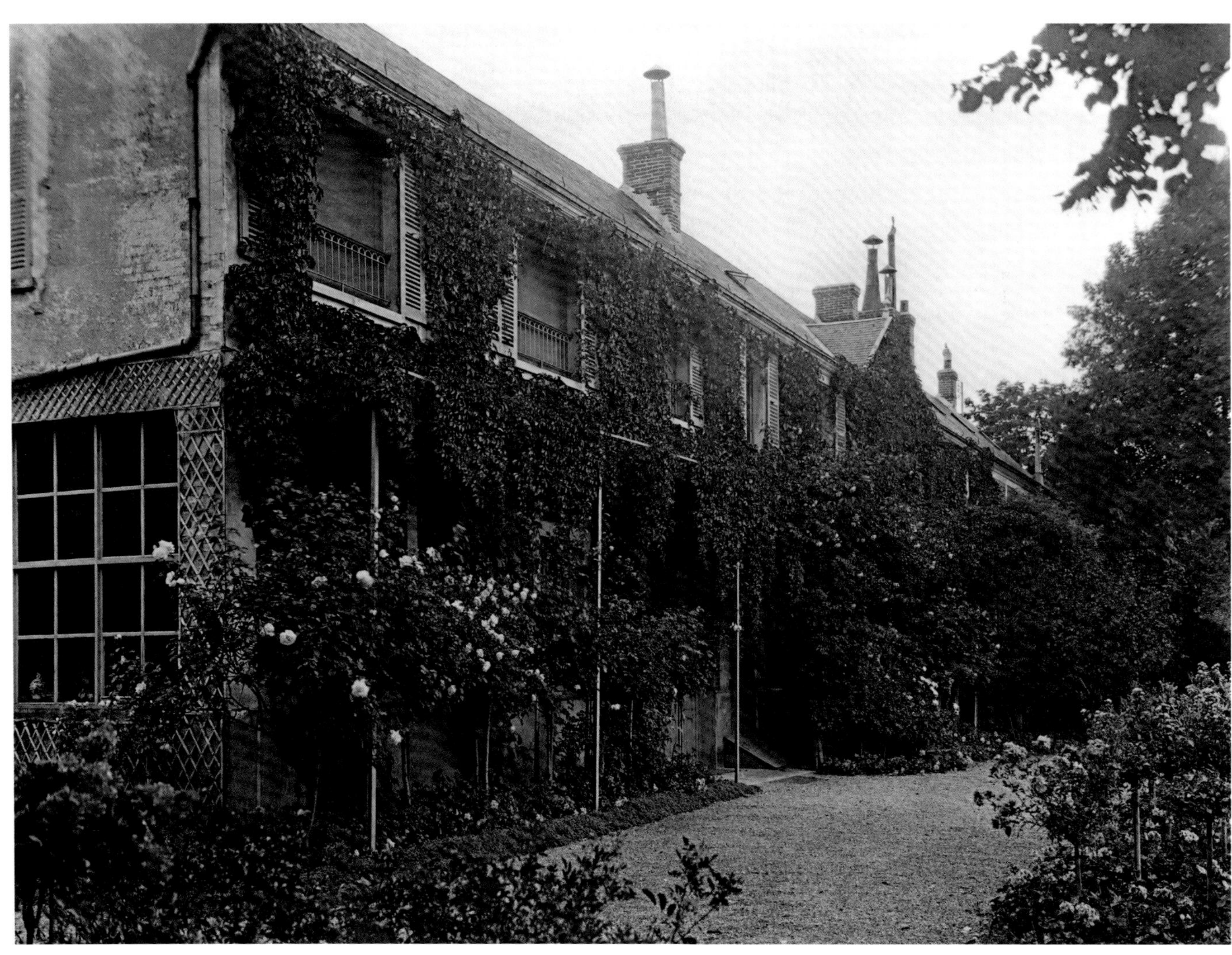

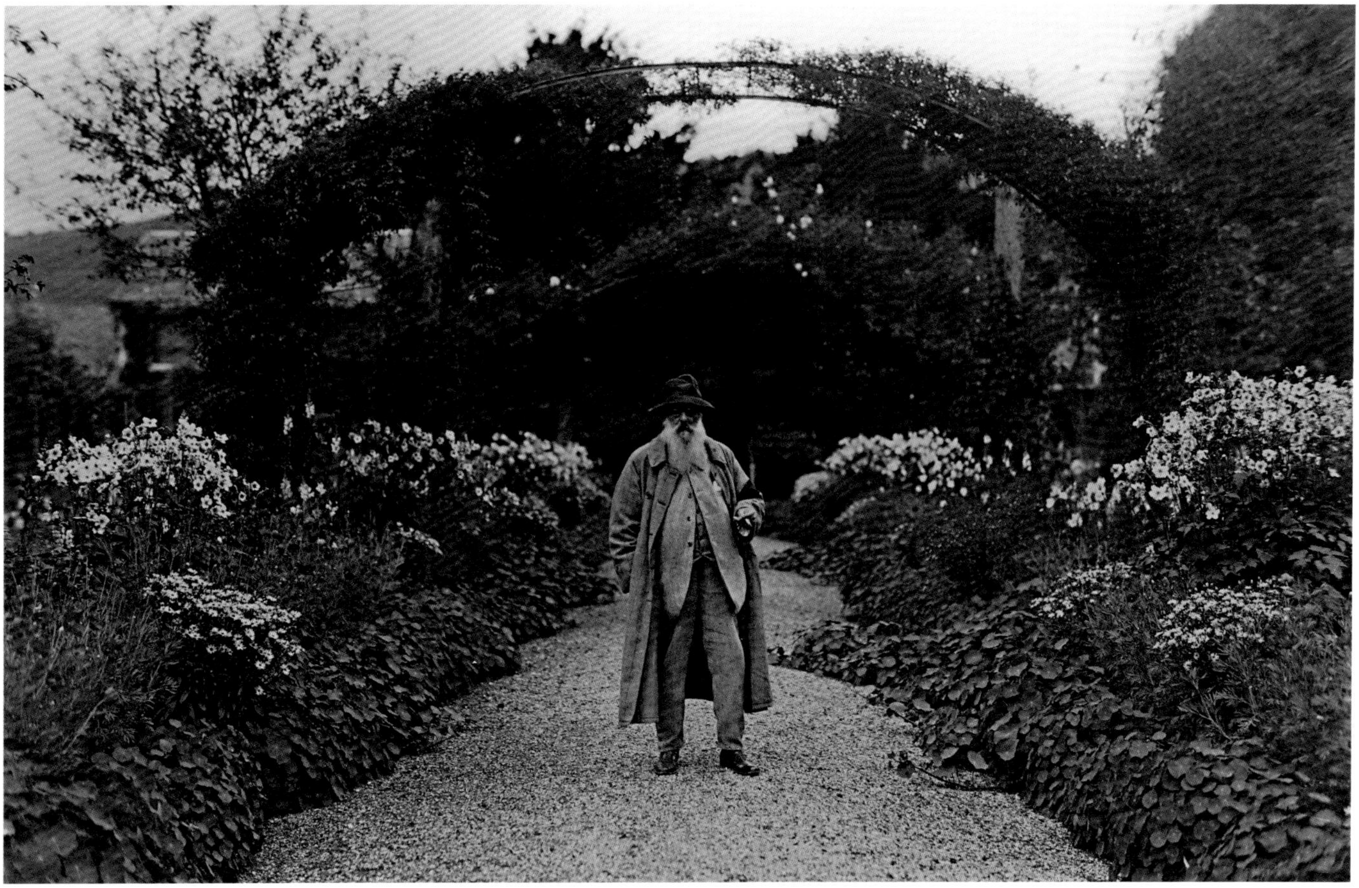

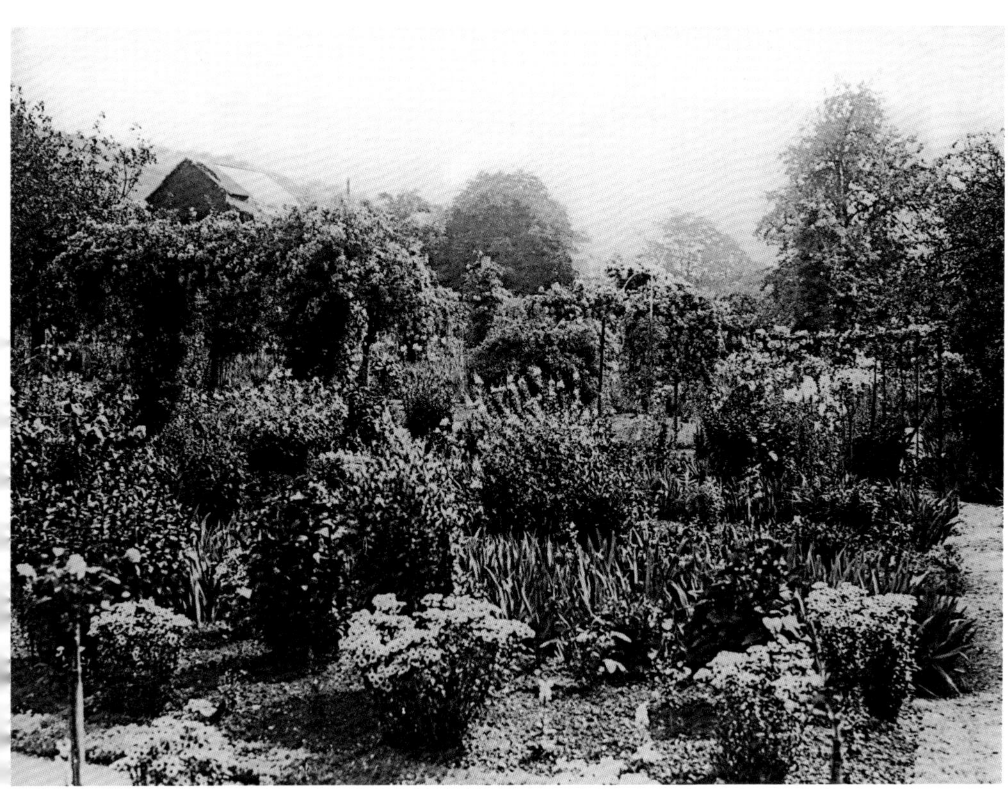

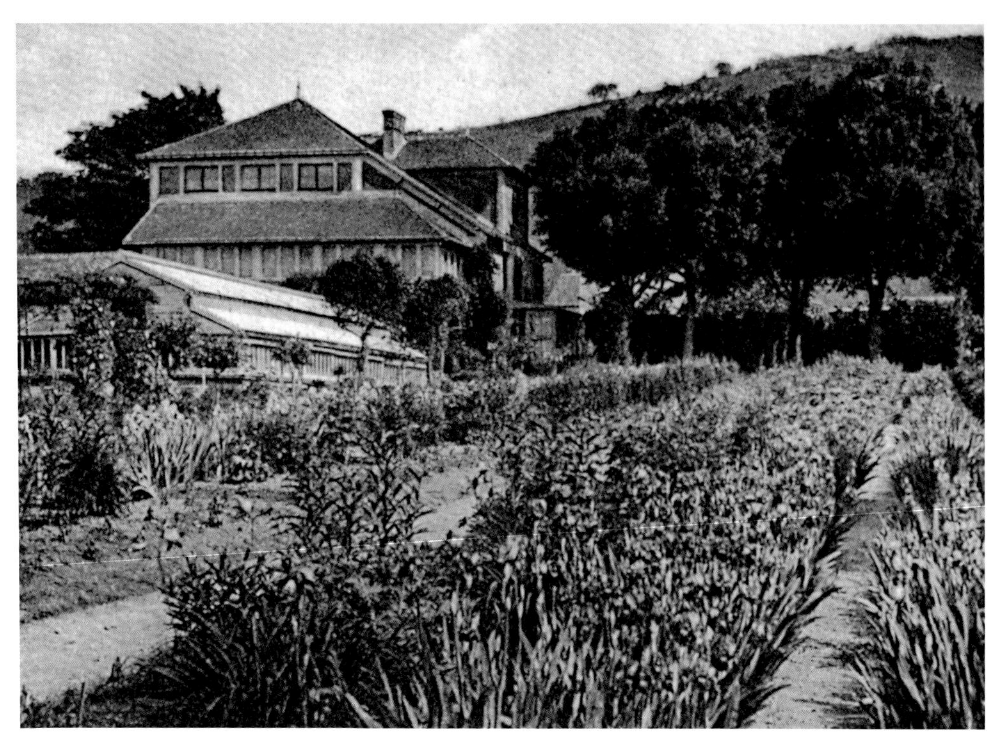

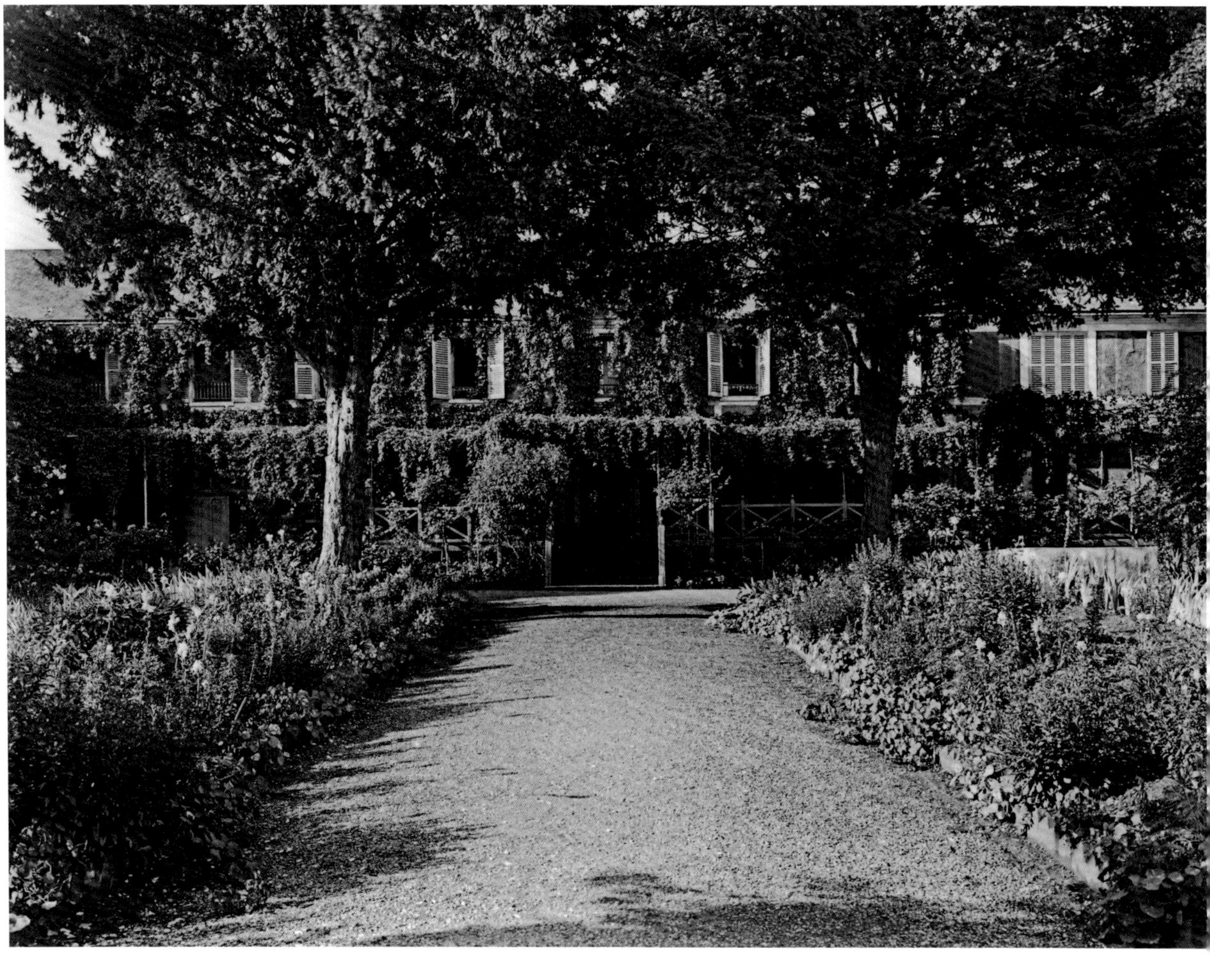

annuals: poppies, sunflowers, and nasturtiums, which he placed around the house and added to the long beds. In the fall he planted scores of daffodil bulbs, and the following spring brought in primroses dug from the woods and clumps of beautiful but invasive willowherb. A visitor described the willowherb's tall shafts of clear pink flowers, which were used at intervals along the back of the main borders.

Within the very French outlines of his garden, a very English style of planting evolved. Giverny was looser, lusher, wilder than most French gardens of the period. In Monet's garden, mullein, a roadside "weed," rubbed shoulders with aristocratic irises and was allowed to self-sow in the flower beds. Instead of filling tidy parterres with solid blocks of a single type of plant, Monet combined a rich variety of annuals, perennials, and biennials with his roses, the backbone of the main borders. And instead of spacing the plants well apart, with earth visible between them, he hid every square inch of ground with foliage and flowers. He even permitted the nasturtiums on either side of the front walk to race toward each other, covering the path and obscuring the straight edges of the beds.

Every year, Monet added more and more flowers to the beds. For a gardener, enough is never enough. Although money was tight, he continued to expand the garden, which he managed on his own with the help of the children. In the late 1880s, his paintings began to sell, first in the United States and then at home. At last, in 1890, he was able to buy the pink house. The proud new owner promptly hired a team of gardeners and started pouring money into the property.

Perhaps because they reminded him of his early years, Monet banished the vegetables to a rented plot at the other end of town so that he could concentrate on his beloved flowers. No longer confined to inexpensive annuals, he collected perennials: irises, peonies, delphiniums, Oriental poppies, asters, and many species of sunflower.

In order to learn about his new plants and their needs, he acquired an impressive botanical library. He sought advice from professional nurserymen, consulted more experienced gardeners, pored over gardening magazines, and attended flower shows. With his close gardening friends Mirbeau and the painter Gustave Caillebotte, he exchanged garden visits and swapped seeds and cuttings. His appetite for plants was insatiable, especially for new and unusual forms and varieties. Like any other gardener, he got carried away and spent a fortune.

The result, though, was unlike any other garden. This was the garden of an artist, who saw the world in terms of color. The flower combinations that had for years been imagined in his paintings came brilliantly to life: exciting juxtapositions of complementary reds and greens, of violets or blues with yellows; of paired primaries: red with yellow, red with blue; and subtle harmonies of closely related hues.

Monet the gardener, influenced perhaps by a spring painting trip to the tulip fields of Holland, developed a series of long, narrow blocks of one or two colors. Alice Kuhn, writing in the women's magazine *La Femme d'aujourd'hui*, described the harmonious hues of the iris in one of these blocks: "Violet-blue, violet-gray, violet–old rose, a few darker violet-brown with gold flecks; violet-purple." The nurseryman Georges Truffaut was struck by the startling contrast of yellow tulips rising in long lines above mats of purple aubretia.

Monet himself rejoiced in both contrast and harmony. For the front of the house, he chose a complementary scheme that he had always loved—tints and shades of red with green. He painted the shutters of the pink house a lovely soft green that came to be called vert Monet, and furnished the island beds with red and pink geraniums, roses, and dianthus. Nature provided the deep-green leaves.

While colorful flowers reigned in the main garden, foliage determined the character of the water garden, which Monet embarked on in 1893. Here, greens predominated, with touches of cool blues, mauves, violets, pinks, and citron yellows. Soft curves replaced the straight lines of the flower gardens.

The site for the water garden was a damp spot across the road from the house, where a tree-lined stream, the Ru, fed a small pond. Wild arrowhead and clumps of native iris studded the grassy banks, and a few yellow and white water lilies floated on the still surface. Monet was entranced by the possibilities of this addition. Water had been the one thing missing from his garden. Now he was content.

From the start, the pond drew him like a magnet, and within a few years, its polished, flower-strewn surface was the center of his life and work. He was fascinated by the floating garden, and hopelessly enamored of water lilies, especially the new hybrids produced by the firm of Marliac. By crossing and recrossing different species, the company founder, Joseph Bory Latour-Marliac, had expanded the color range to include delicious shades of red, pink, purple, and lavender. How could Monet resist? In 1904, he ordered 'Arethusa,' 'Atropurpurea,' and 'James Brydon,' the last a stunning deep-pink variety still available from nursery catalogues.

He also ordered water-loving grasses and numerous species of bog iris. The head gardener, Félix Breuil, who was in charge of the water garden, wrote an article about the irises for Jardinage, enumerating the many species growing at Giverny. His list included a Siberian iris, 'Snow Queen,' which was first brought to Europe from the Far East in 1900, and which I grow in my garden.

Much as he loved irises, water lilies remained Monet's favorite aquatic plants. By the turn of the century, he had painted them innumerable times, and in 1909, paintings of water lilies were featured in a major exhibition. Far from losing their charm, they drew him deeper and deeper into their own mysterious world, where water and sky, illusion and reality, painter and subject, became one.

Under their spell, he entertained a novel idea. As he told an interviewer, "The temptation came to me to use this water-lily theme for the decoration of a drawing room: carried along the walls, enveloping all the partitions with its unity, it would have produced the illusion of an endless whole, of a wave with no horizon and no shore; nerves exhausted by work would have relaxed there . . . and to anyone who would have lived in it, that room would have offered a refuge of peaceful meditation in the middle of a flowering aquarium."

Years later, Monet's dream of this "endless whole" became a reality. Only months before his death, he completed twenty-two huge panels in which he captured forever the fleeting glories of his watery world. He did not live to see this great work installed in the Musée de l'Orangerie, but his gardener of thirty years did. According to Vivian Russell in *Monet's Garden*: Félix Breuil "never went back to look at his pond. He went instead to visit it in the Orangerie."

Today, water lilies continue to float on the pond at Giverny. In May, irises in every imaginable shade of blue and violet bloom in their long, narrow beds; in June, roses smother the metal arches along the front walk. By midsummer, gladioli stand tall among the nasturtiums, which have begun their headlong rush toward the middle of the path. And in the fall, dahlias lavish their rich colors on the beds. The gardens, now open to the public, are the property of the Académie des Beaux-Arts. But Claude Monet still owns them.

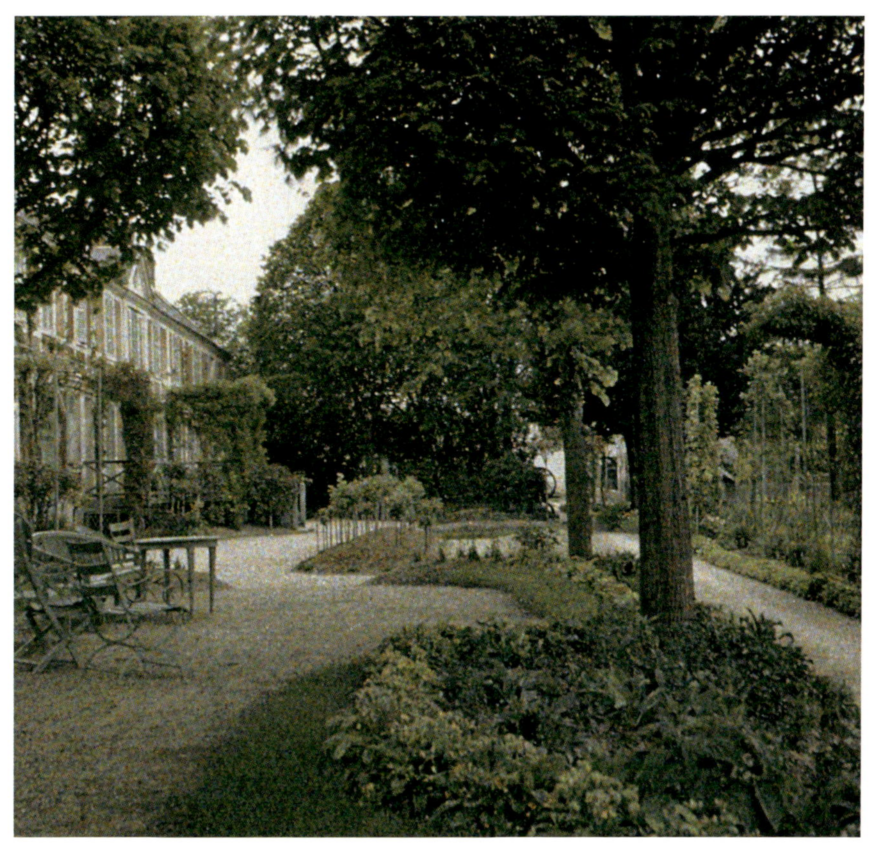

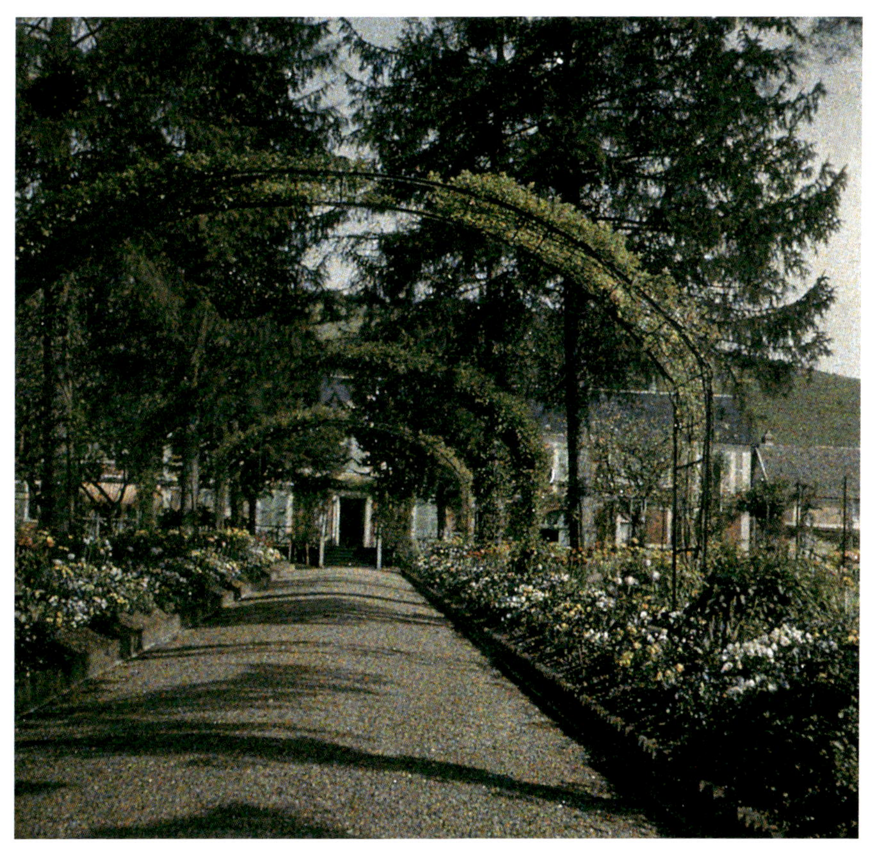

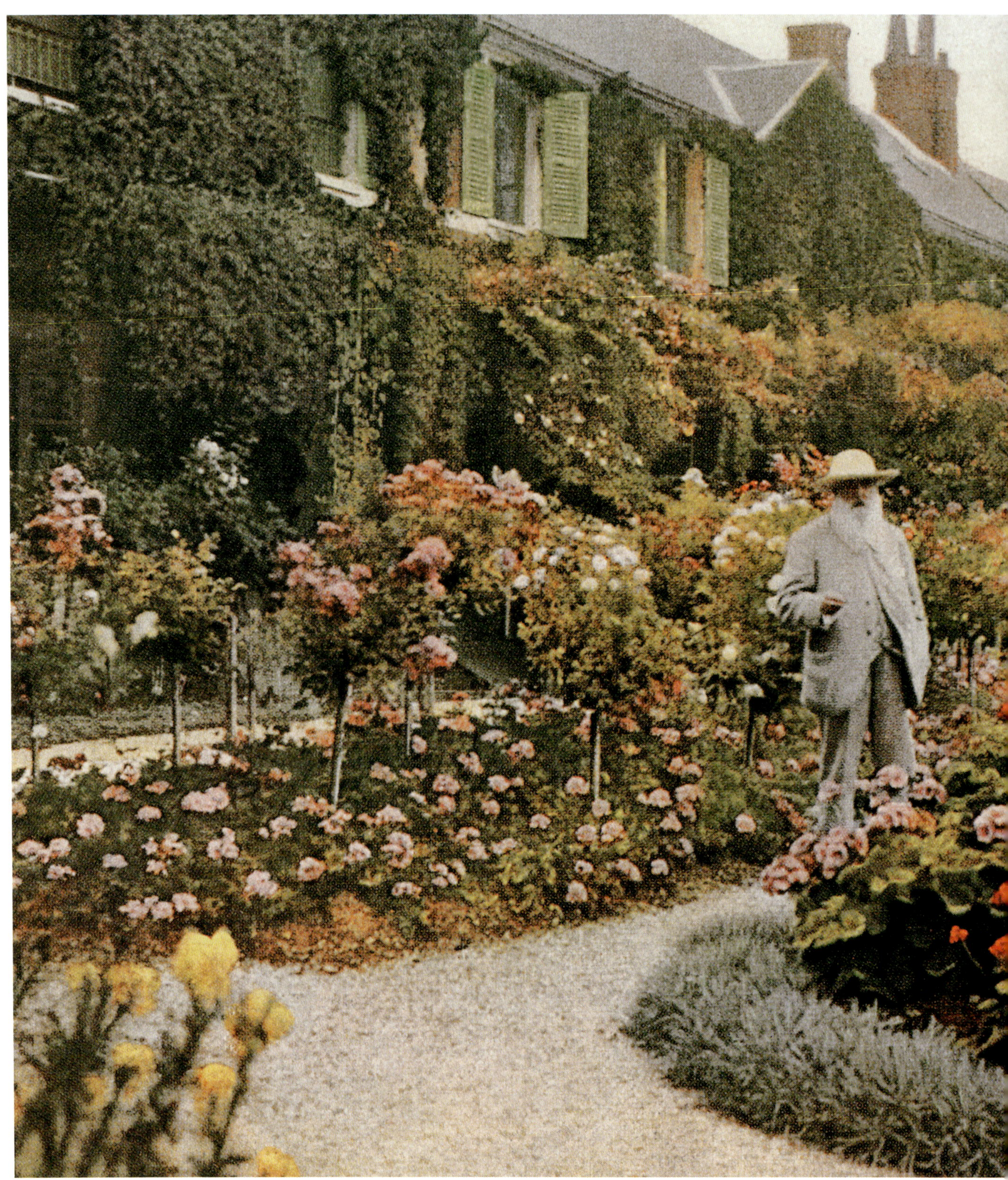

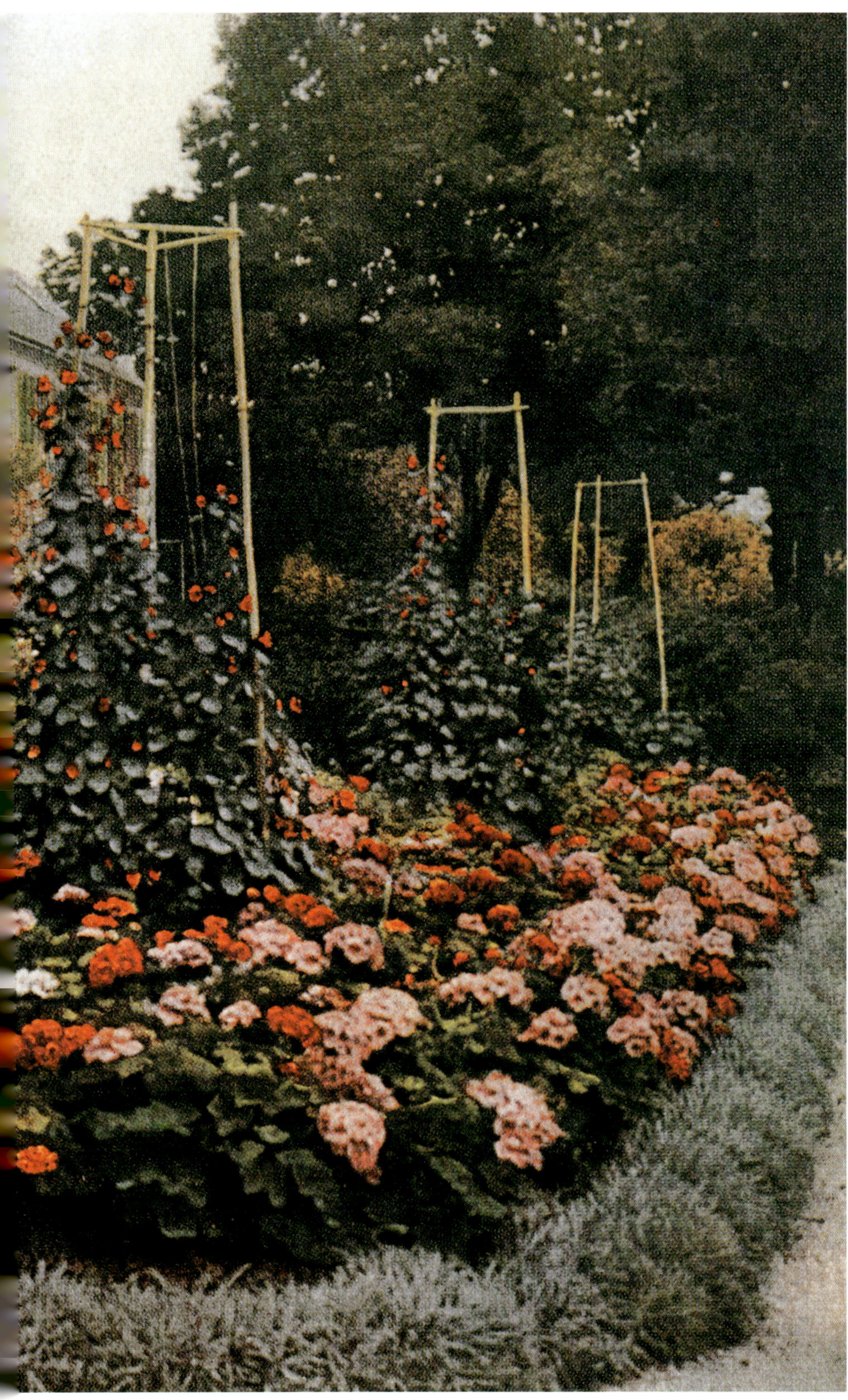

Over the years, Monet's taste in flowers grew increasingly sophisticated, but he never abandoned old favorites; he continued to fill his front beds with geraniums or, more correctly, pelargoniums.

True geraniums are hardy perennials, rejoicing in the common name "cranesbill," which derives from *geranos*, Greek for "crane." Monet's geraniums were frost-tender perennials from South Africa whose botanical name, *Pelargonium*, comes from the Greek *pelargos*, or "stork."

The seeds of those two genera are thought to resemble the long beaks of the respective birds. The real difference between the two lies in the arrangement of petals. While geranium petals are evenly spaced, pelargoniums feature an arrangement suggestive of pansies, two larger petals above a trio of smaller ones. Fine distinctions aside, the handsome flower clusters of the pelargoniums are by far the showiest.

THE GARDEN PATH

Paths play a central role in the design of any garden. They divide and conquer space, link the house to different parts of the property, and determine the style of the garden. Depending on their function and the choice of surfacing material, paths can be formal or informal, whimsical or utilitarian, but all must arrive at a destination, whether it is the garage or a secluded garden bench.

According to the Connecticut garden designer Betty Ajay, access paths should be short, straight, and to the point. They should make it possible to walk, dry-shod and in safety, to the front door. The English writer Hugh Johnson would agree. In his book *The Principles of Gardening*, he cites the French suggestion for designing a curving path: "Get your gardener drunk and follow his footsteps." A meandering path does in fact serve a purpose, intentionally slowing the pace of foot traffic and inviting the wanderer to linger and look.

From the garden gate to the front door, Monet employed the most direct route and straight lines, though softened by a sprawl of nasturtiums. But the paths in his water garden curved among trees and shrubs and skirted the pond, leading visitors to the Japanese footbridge and the best views of the water lilies.

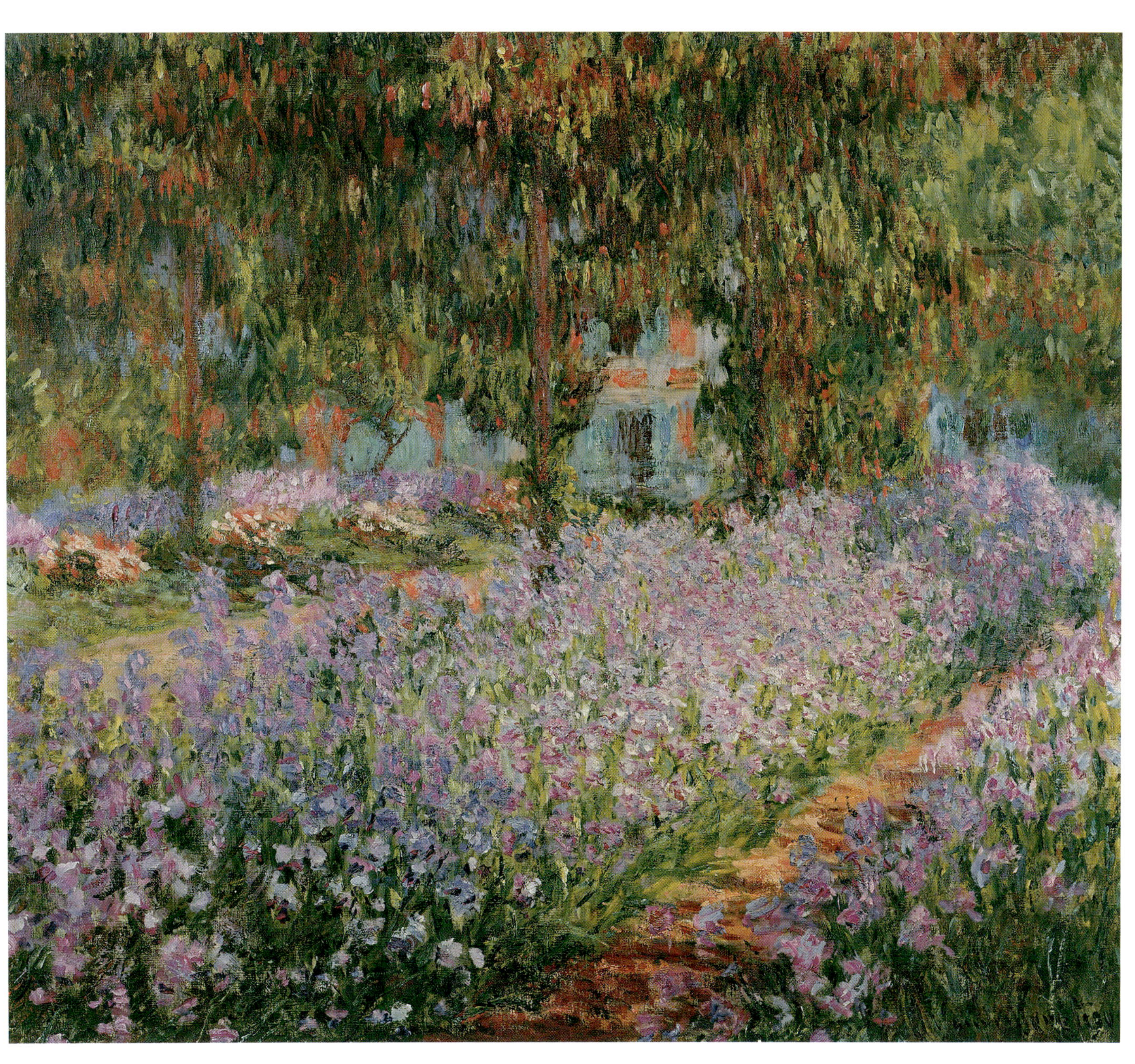

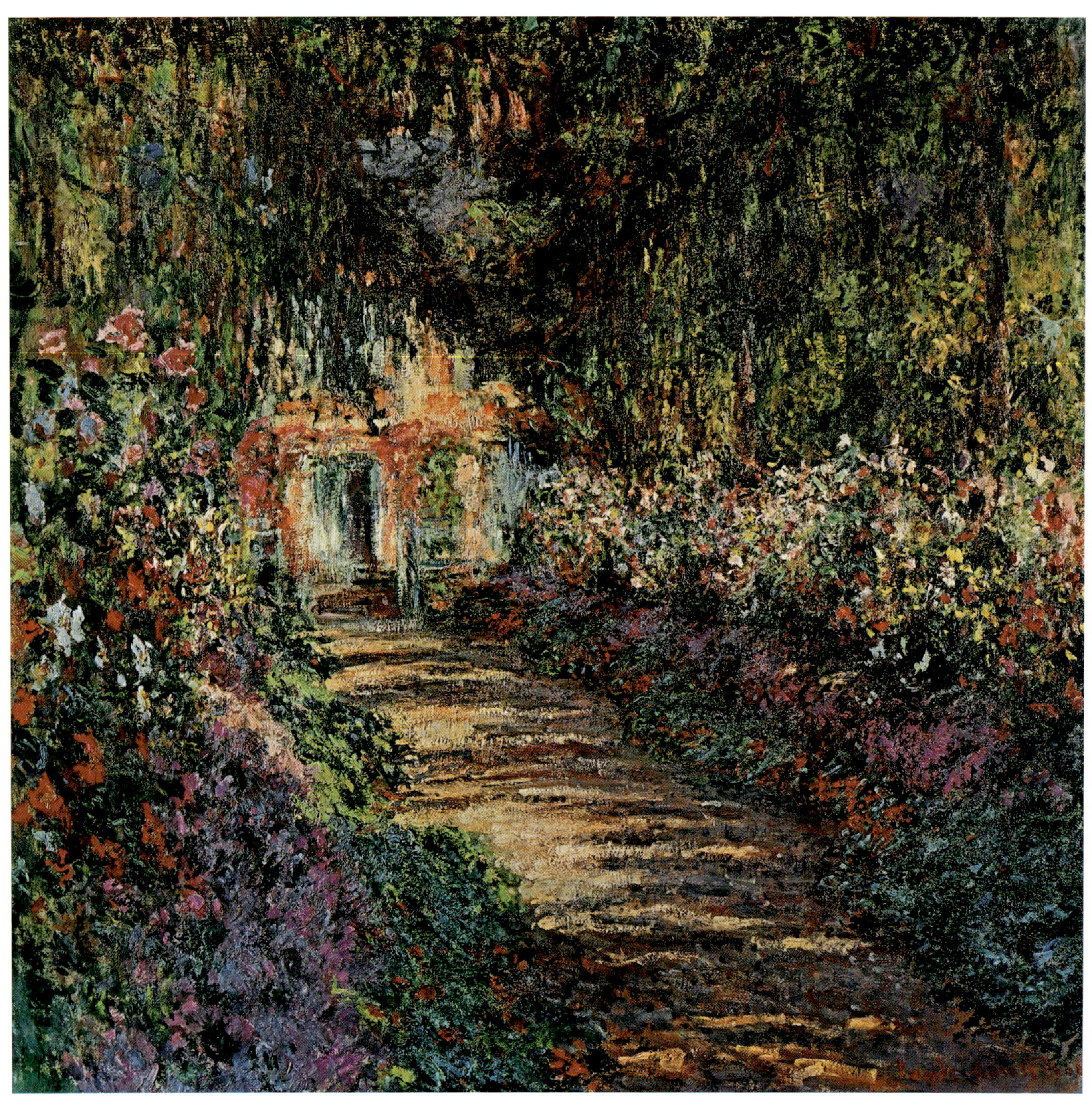

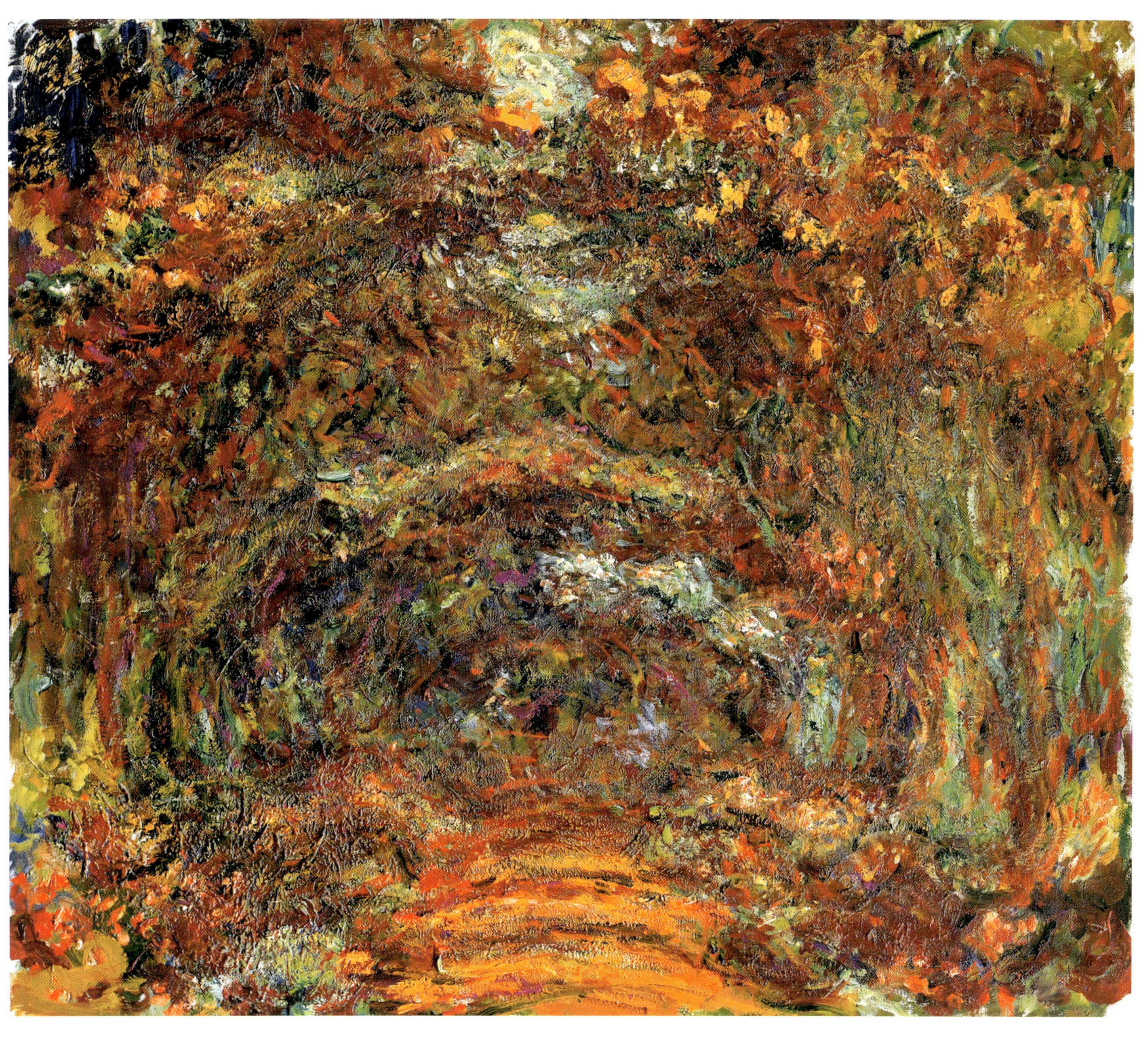

THE WATER GARDEN

Although the two gardens are often described in very different terms and have been viewed by most Monet authors as separate, they were two distinct but crucial elements of a passionate ensemble. Both required considerable thought on the part of Monet, in close consultation with his head gardener, as well as the expense of tremendous energy by a team of six full-time assistants, who were instrumental in achieving the painter's seasonal orchestration of colors and forms. The flower garden, although composed of rather strict beds, was nonetheless lyrical in texture, color, and effusion. Monet's extensive knowledge allowed him to achieve year after year a floral chorus of constantly changing pitch, sweep, and complexity. Across the way, in the water garden, the elements were fewer, and blended together in subtle harmony. The artist masterfully created a luxurious tapestry fusing water lilies, willows, light, and reflections. It was his private world, an open-air studio open to nature. Monet's friend Gustave Geffroy wrote this about the water garden in the final chapter of his biography of the painter: "There he found, so to speak, the last word of things, if things have a first and a last word. He discovered and demonstrated that *everything* is *everywhere,* and that after running around the world worshipping the light that illuminates it, he knew that this light came to be reflected with all its splendors and mysteries in the magical hollow surrounded by the foliage of willows and bamboo, by flowering iris and rosebushes, through the mirror of water from which burst the strange flowers, which seem more silent and more hermetic than all the others."

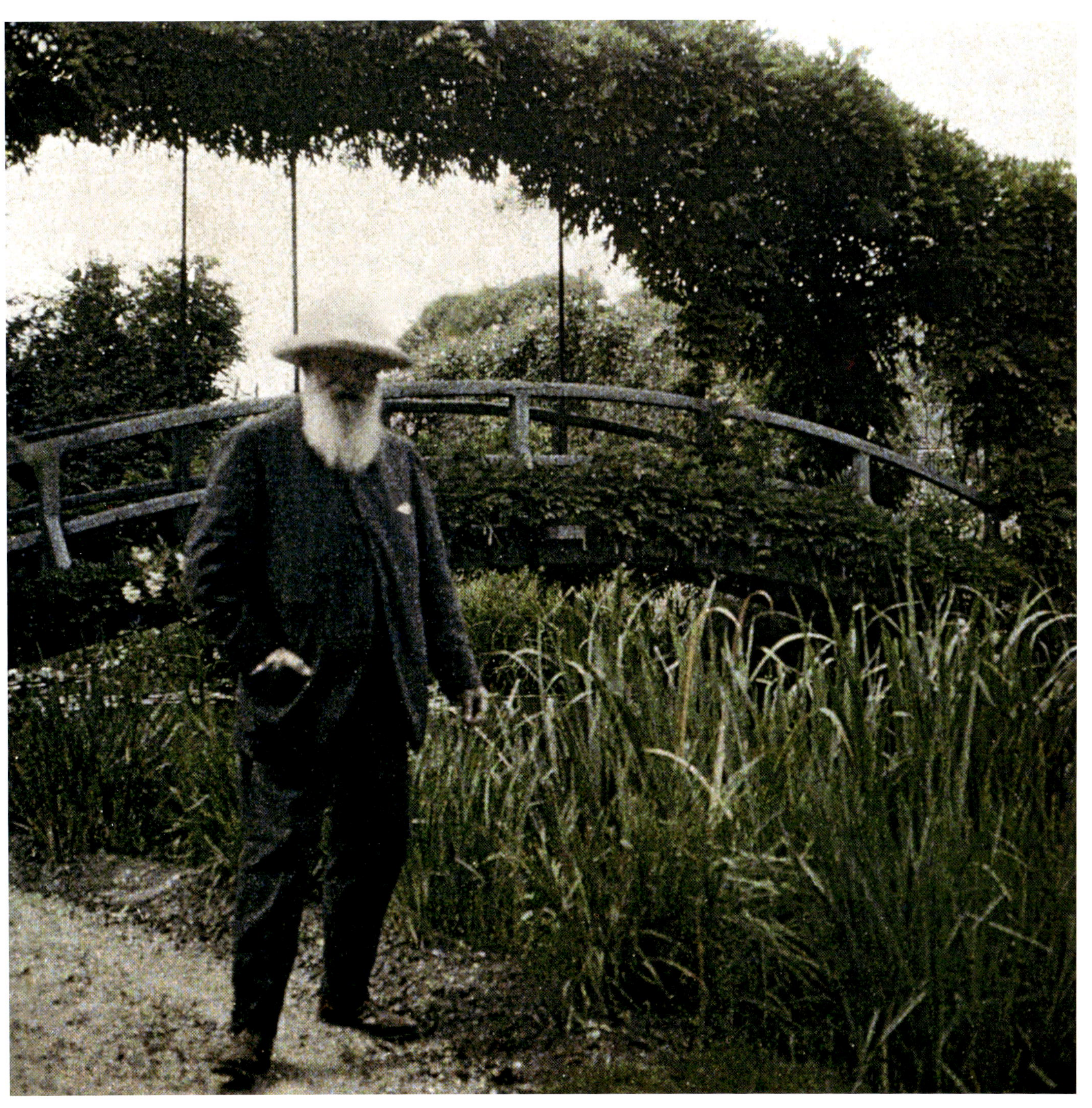

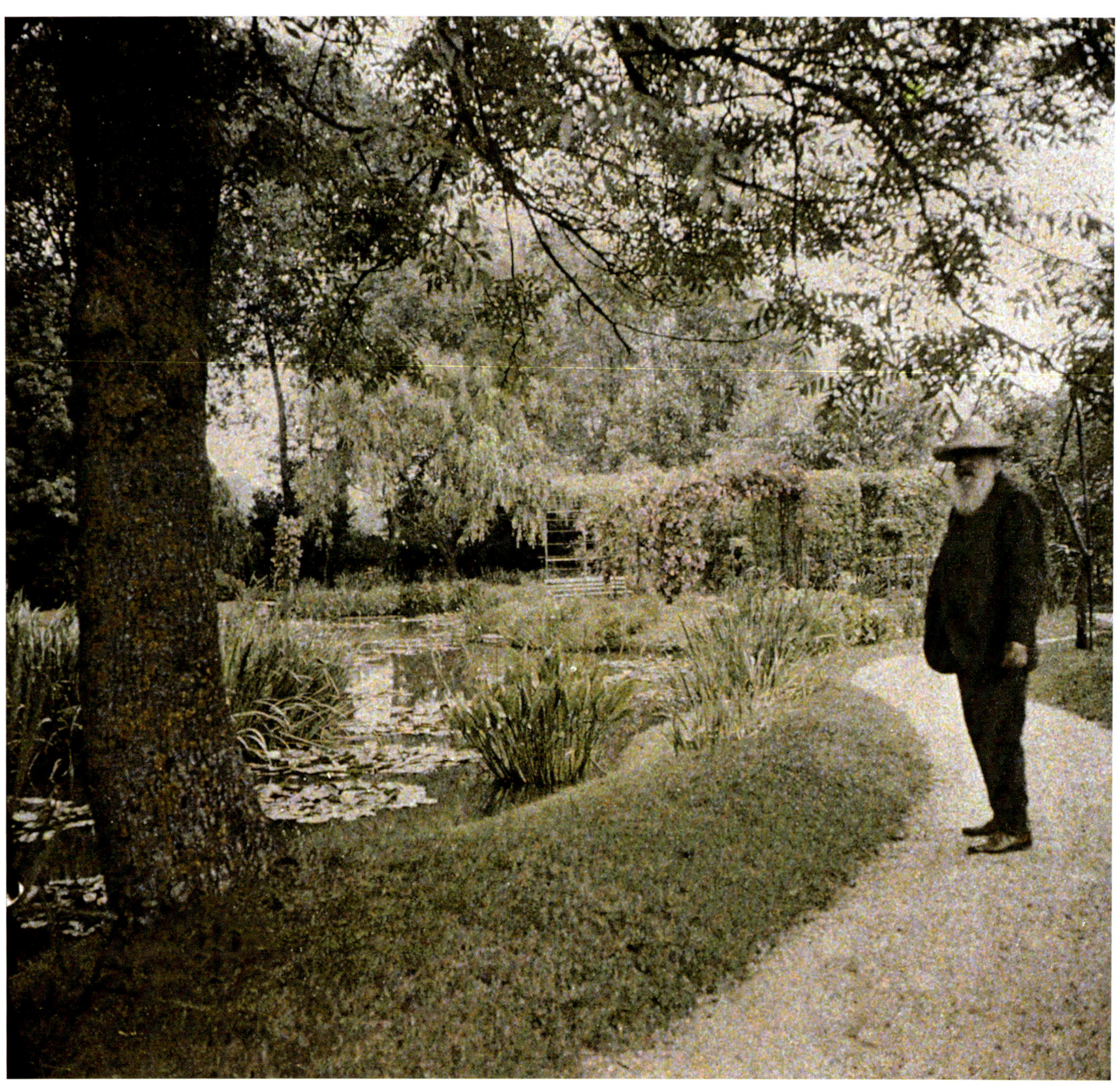

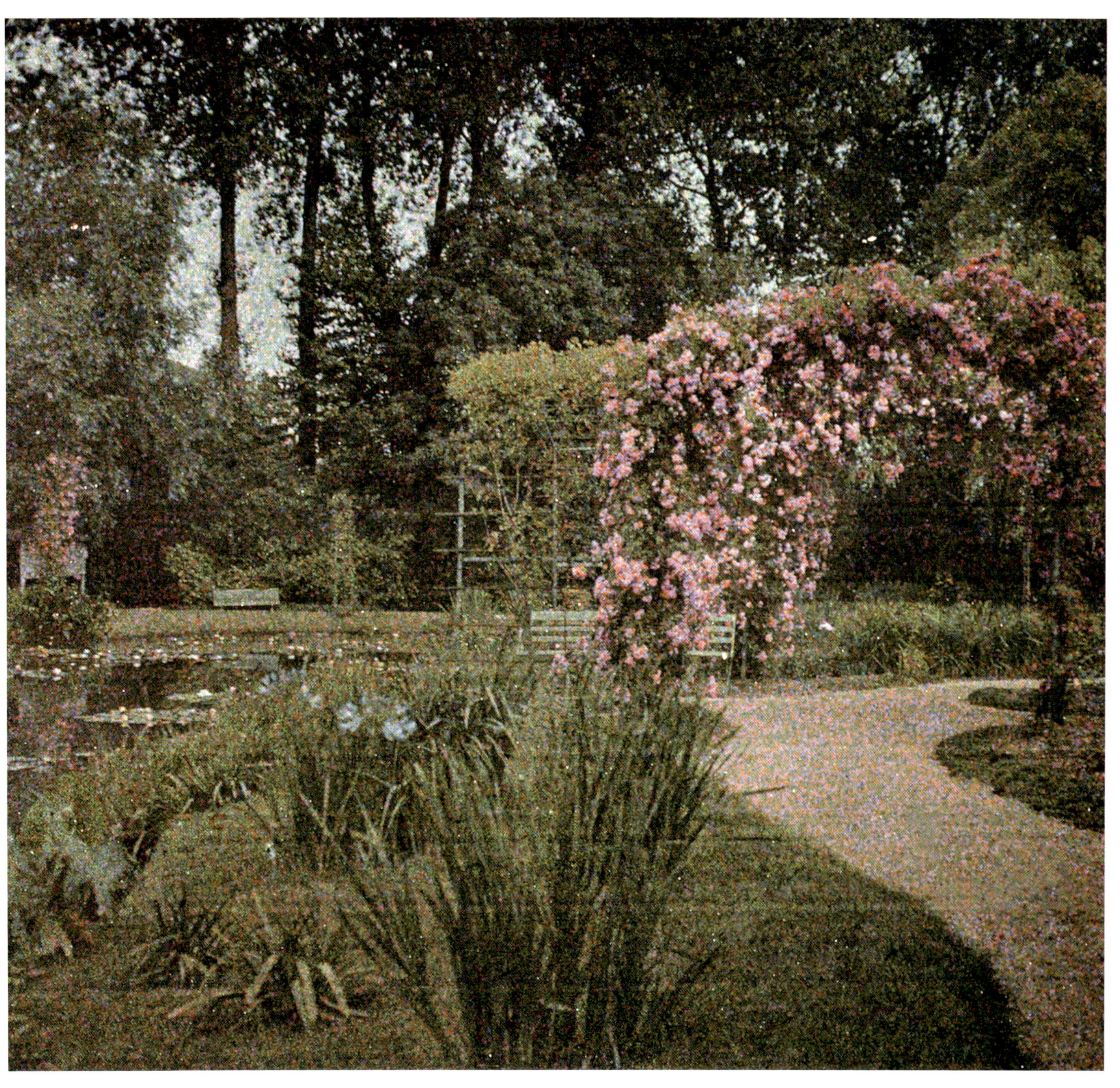

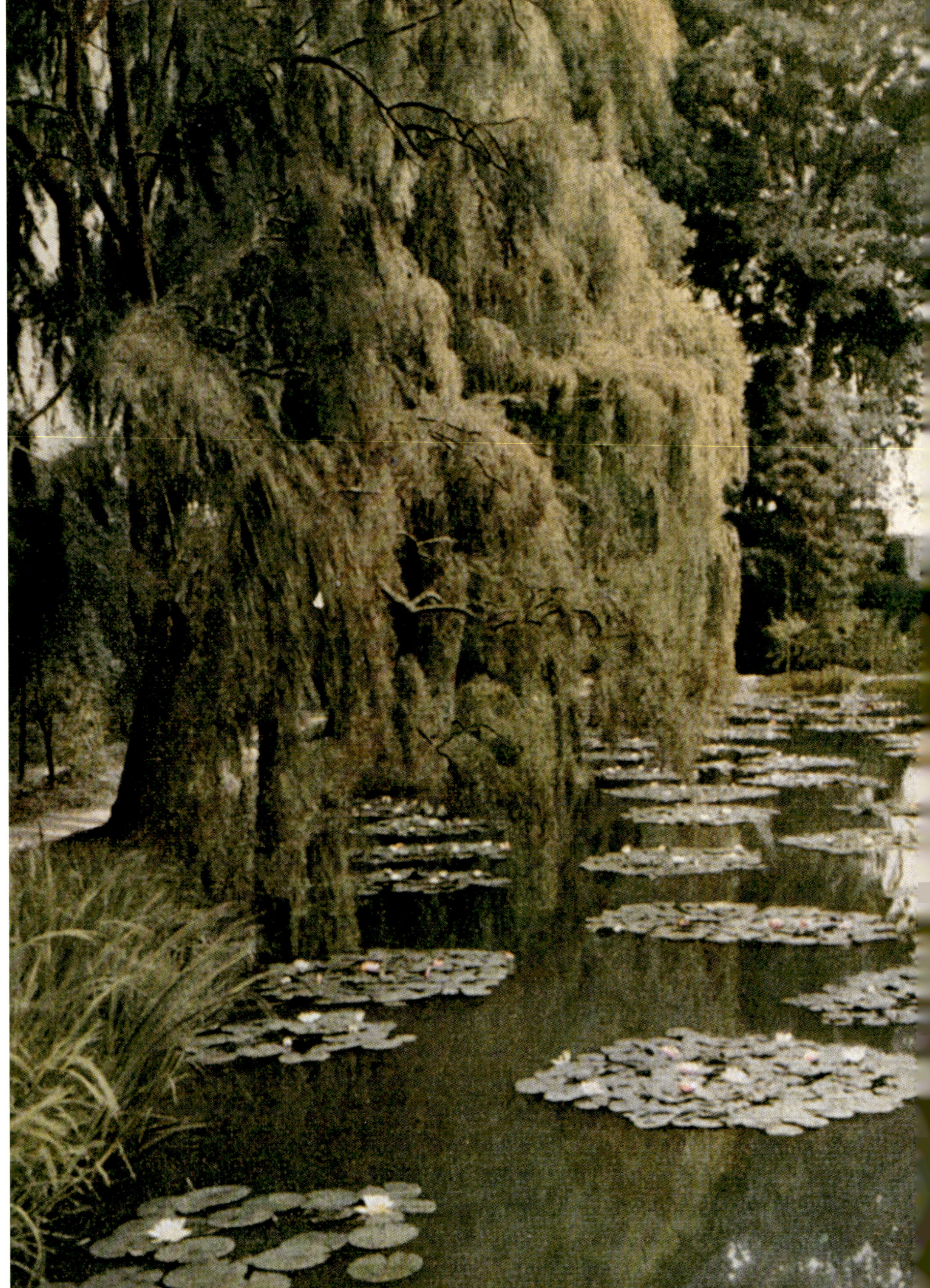

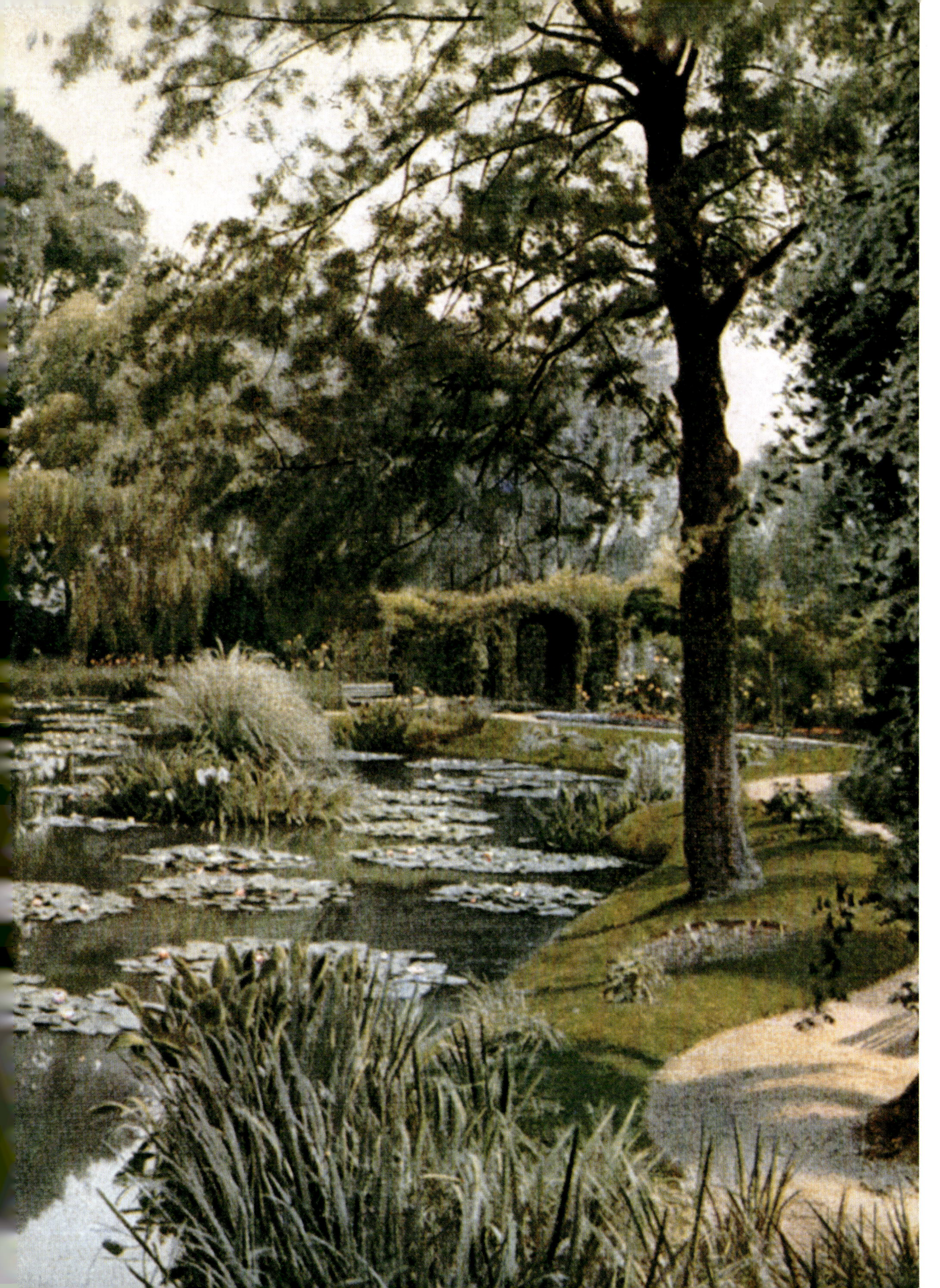

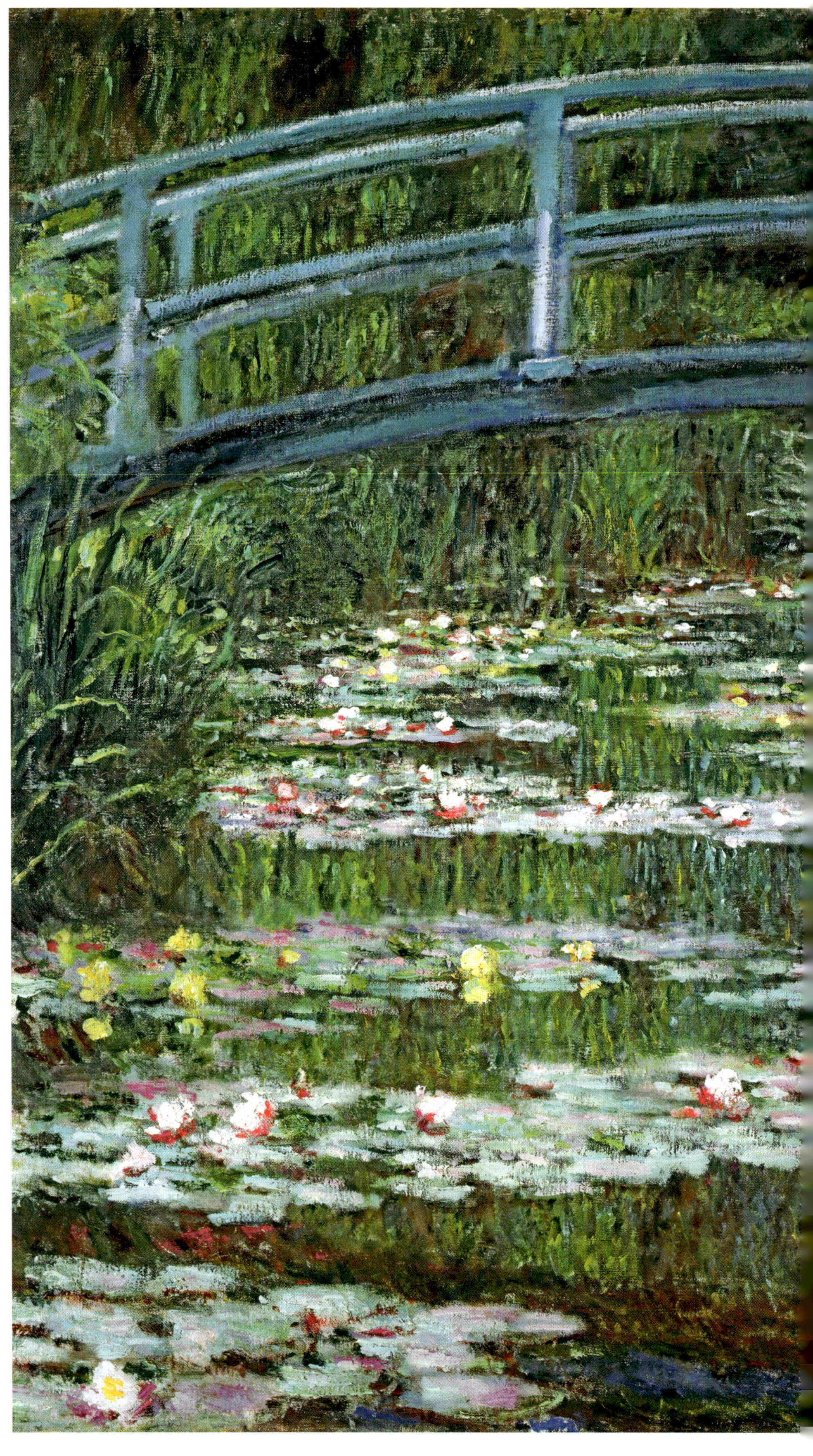

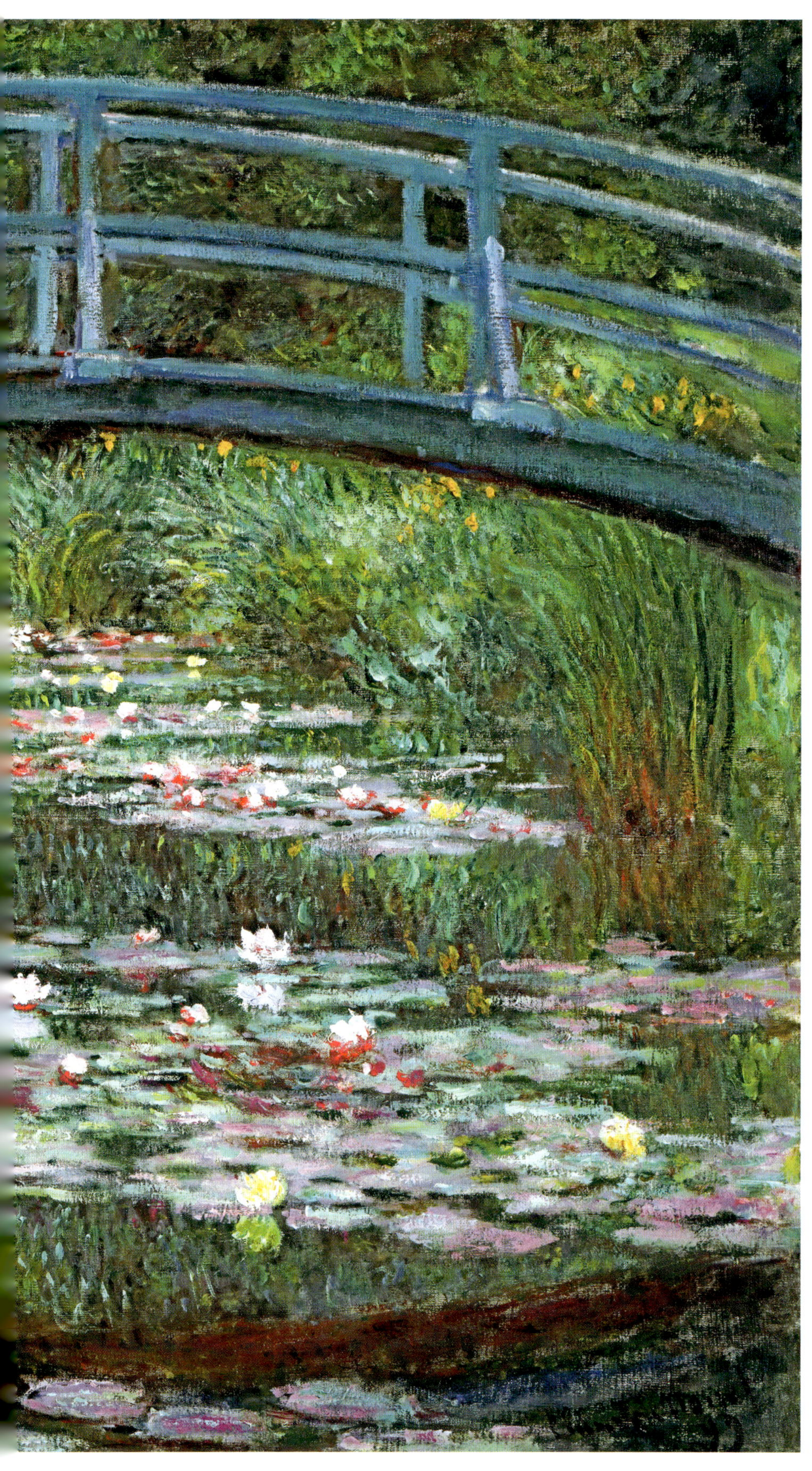

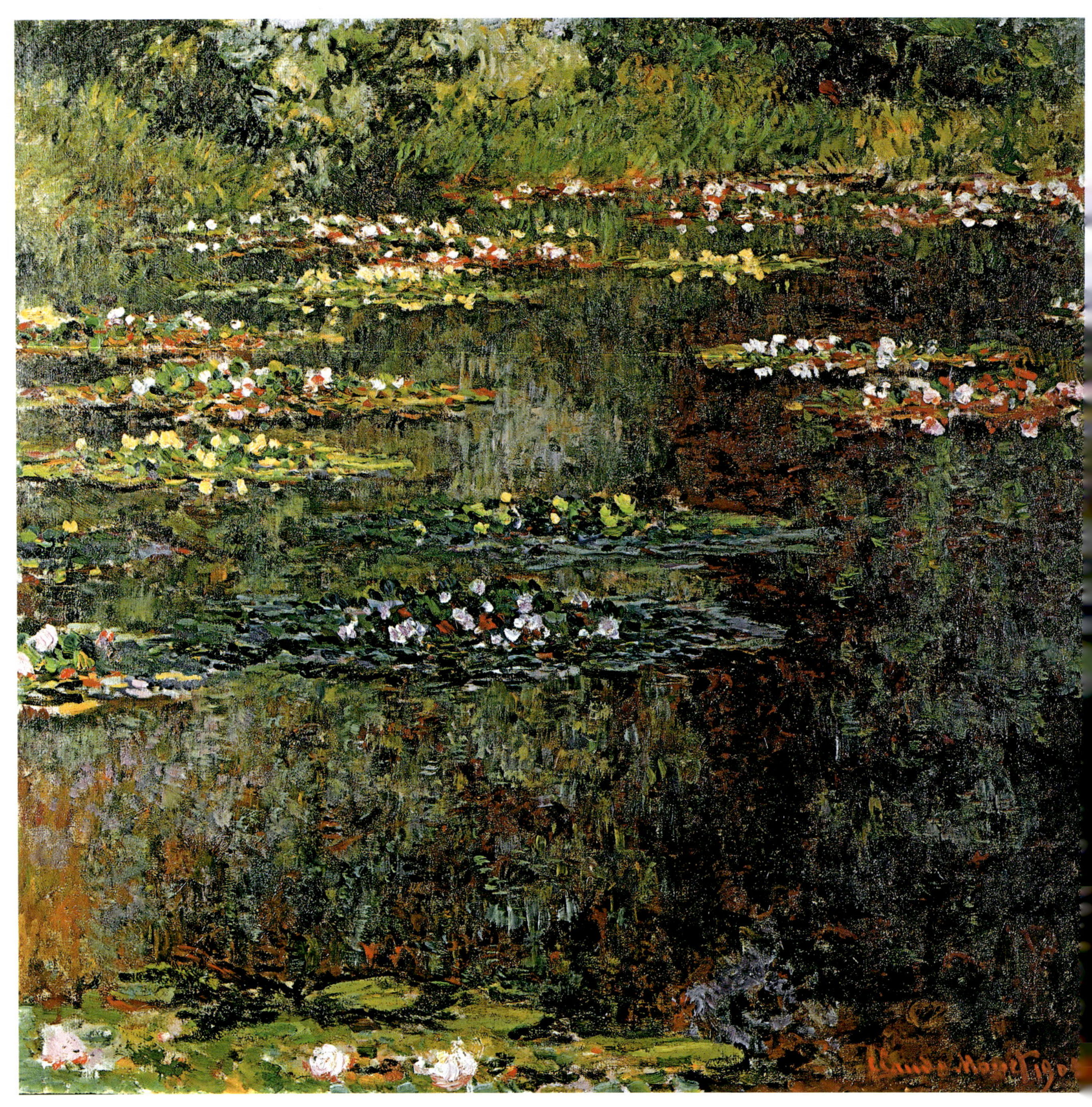

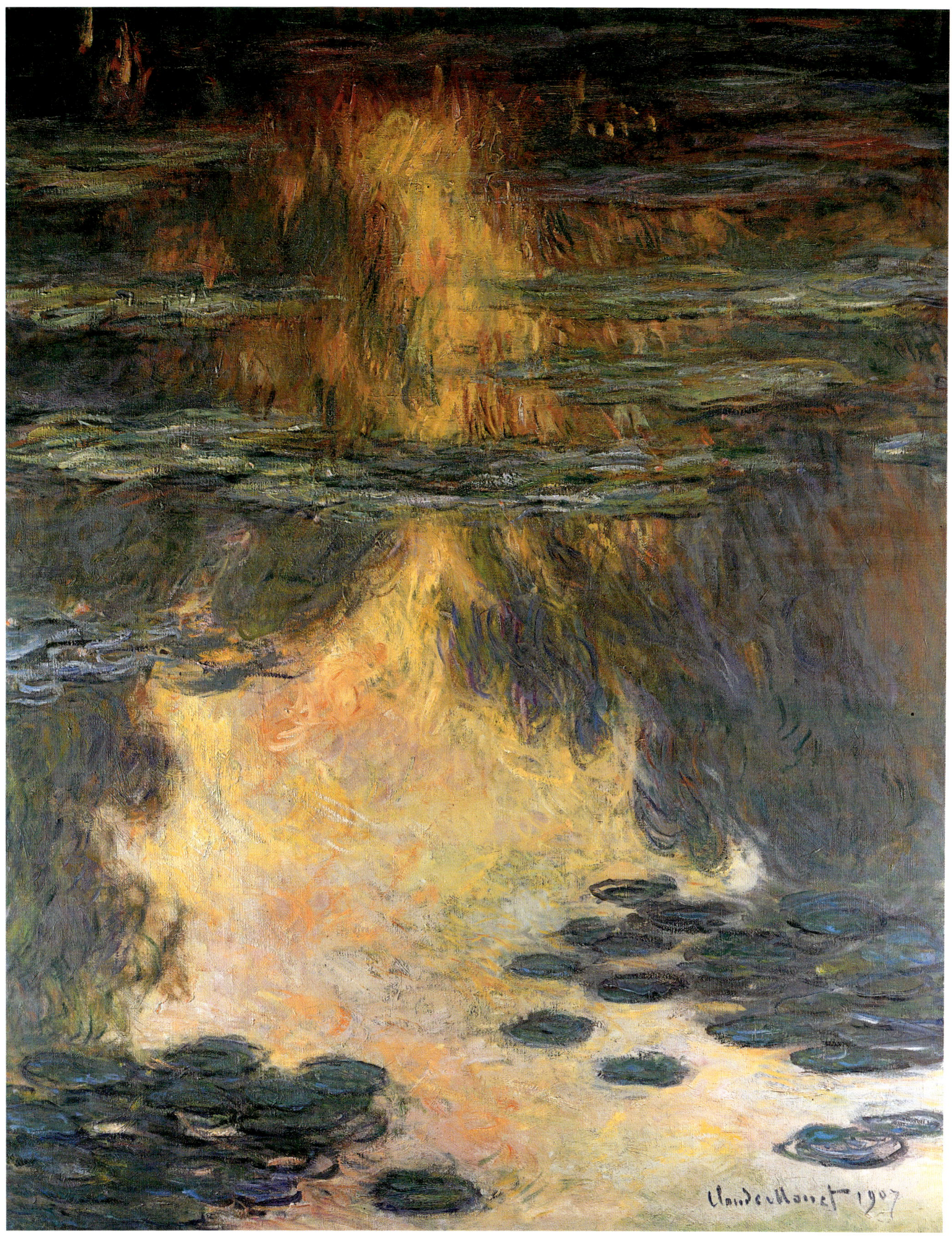
Claude Monet 1907

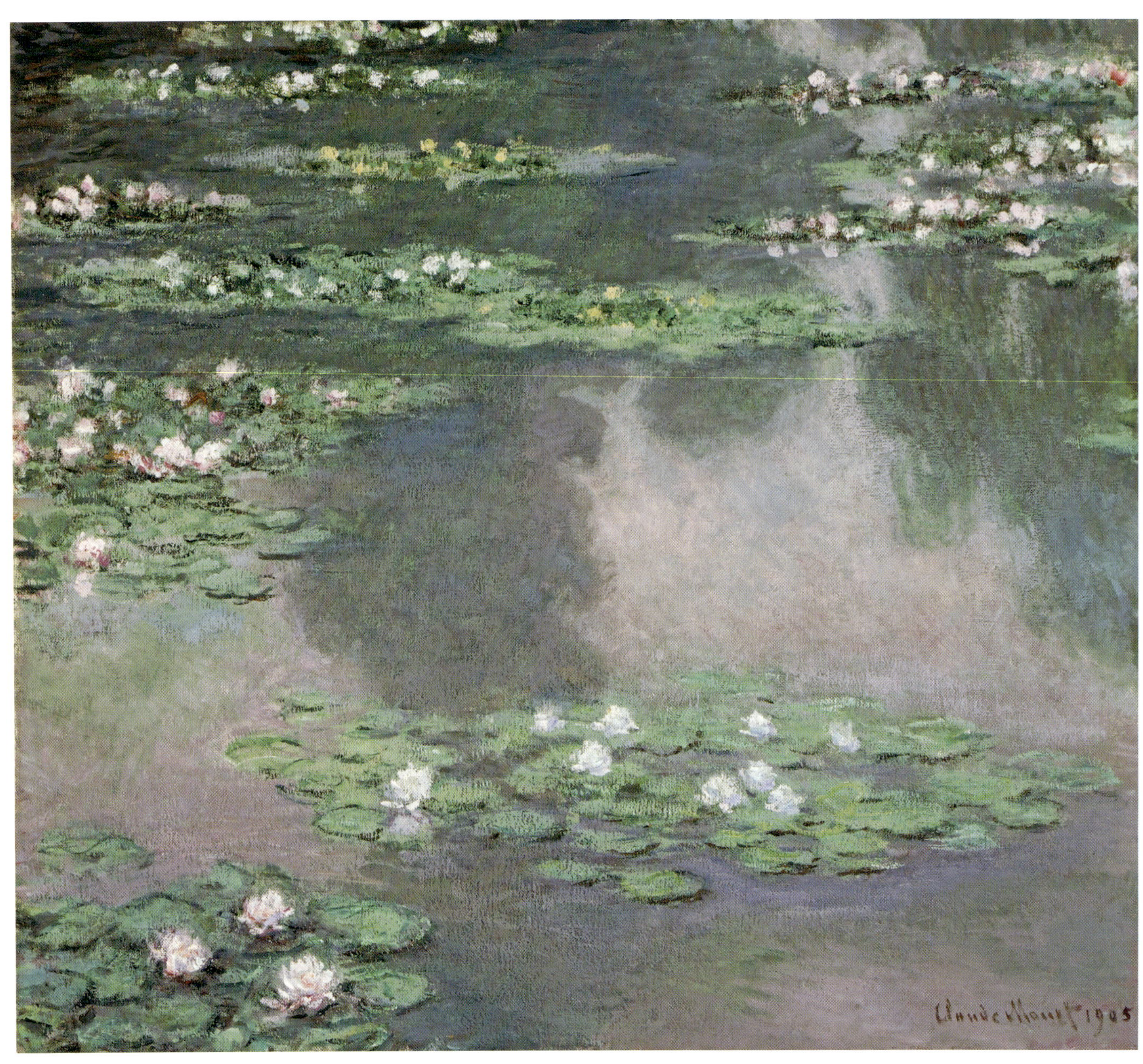
Claude Monet 1905

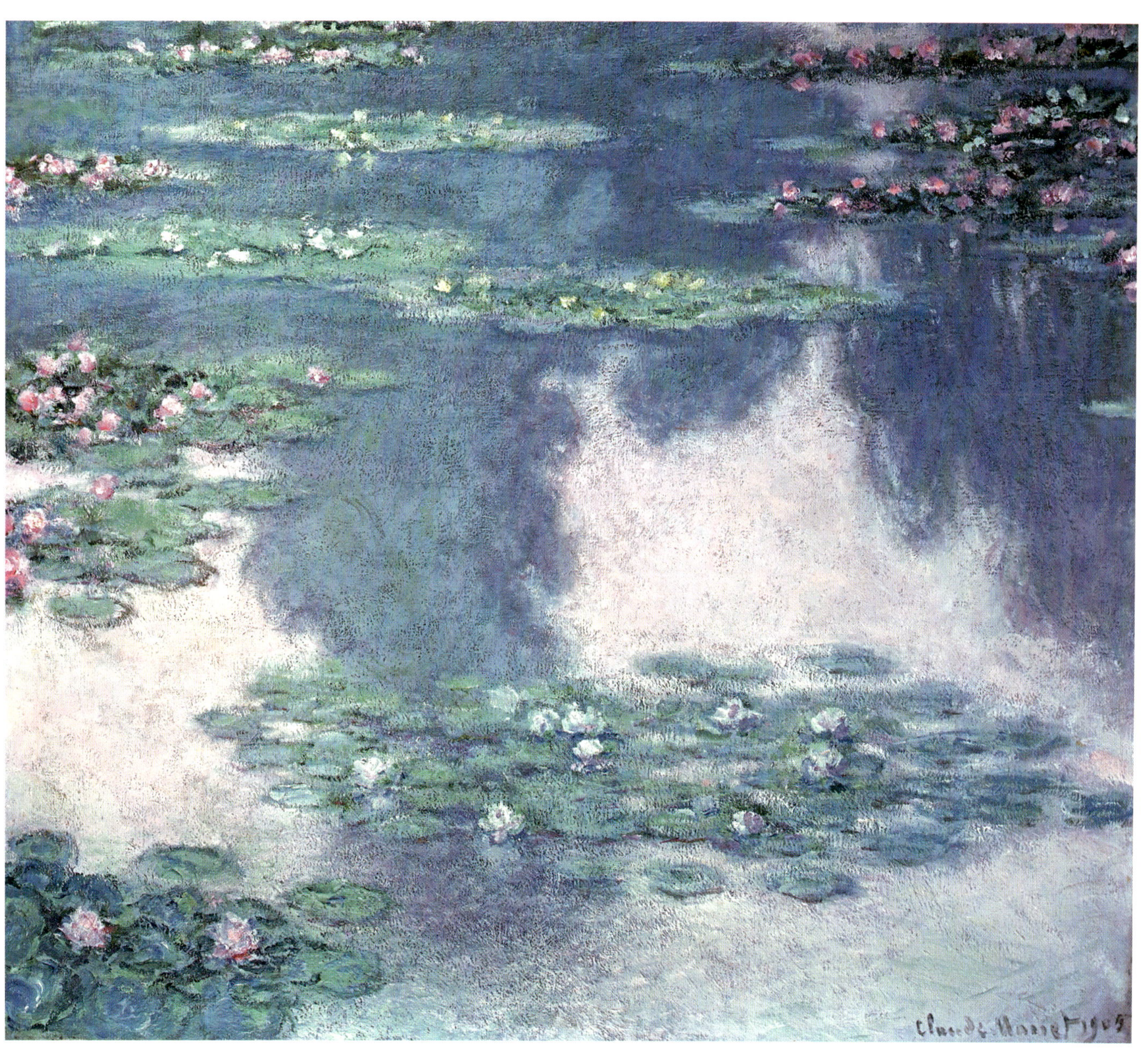

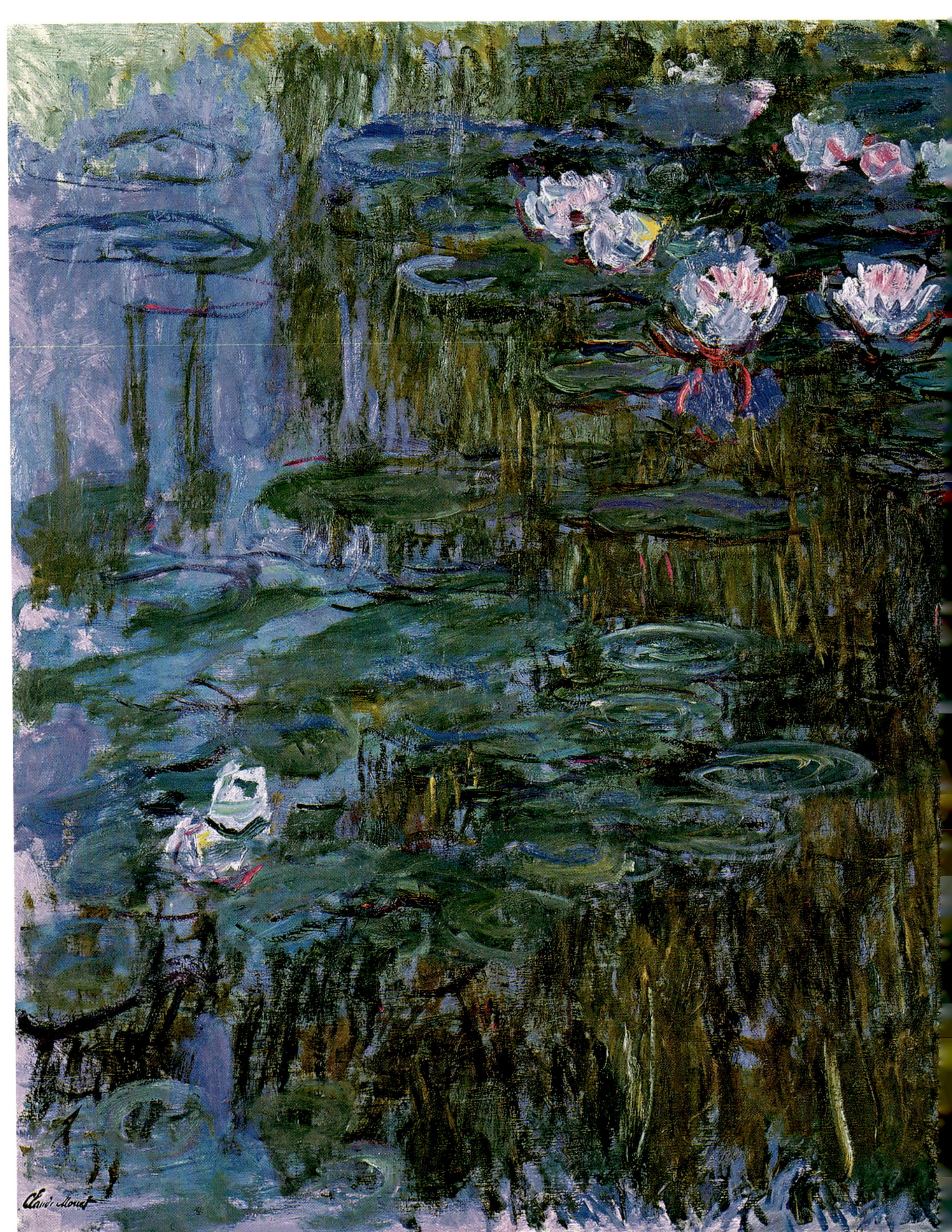

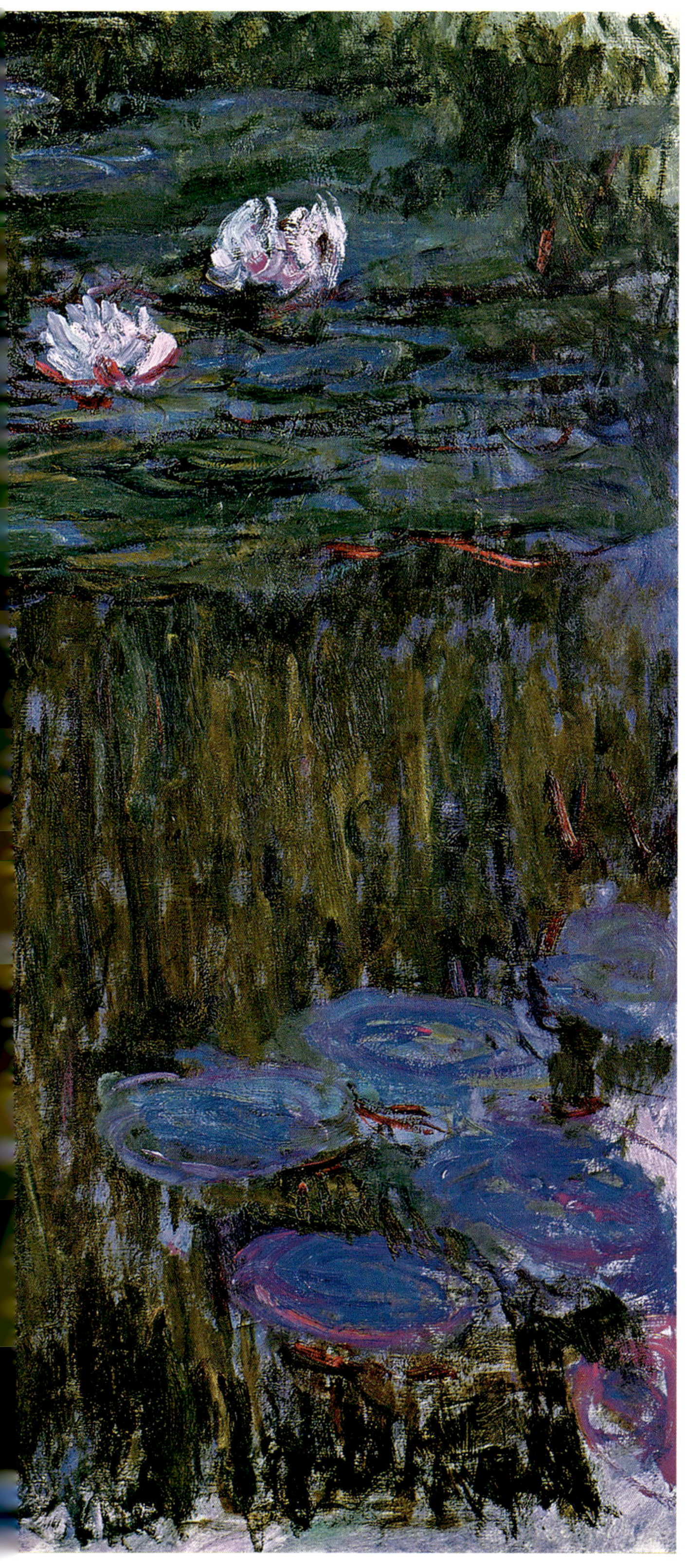

(overleaf) By all accounts, Monet had a particular affinity for blue flowers, and he satisfied his craving for the color by planting hundreds of South African agapanthus . It is a measure of his regard for the beautiful blue umbellate flowers that the tuberous roots had to be dug up every fall, wintered in the greenhouse, and returned to their outdoor homes in the spring.

At the edge of the water-lily pond, agapanthus rubbed shoulders with wild blue-flag irises and yellow *Iris pseudacorus;* with common wildflowers such as marsh marigolds and meadow rue; with grasses, both indigenous and exotic; and with the huge, round platelike leaves of petasites.

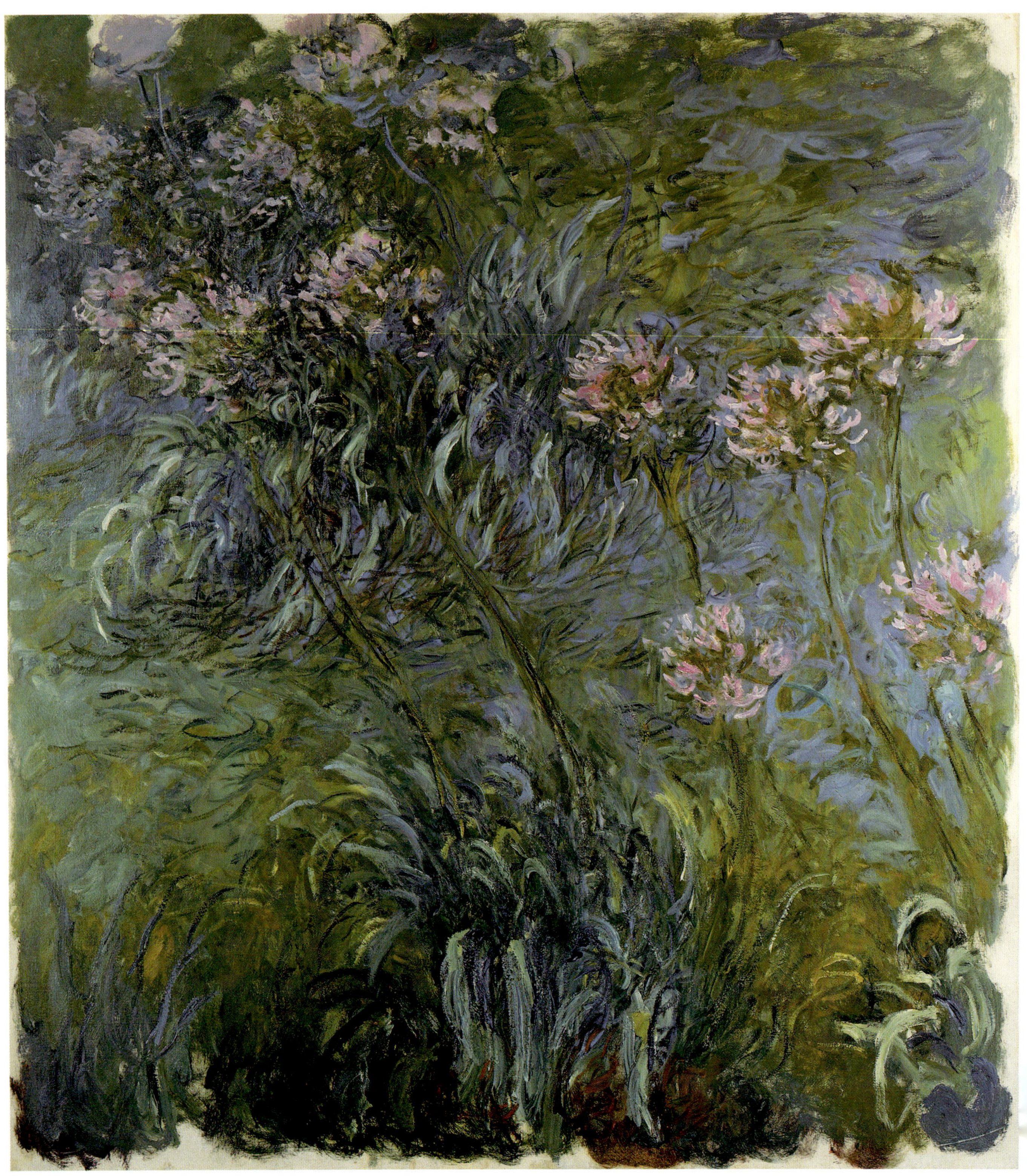

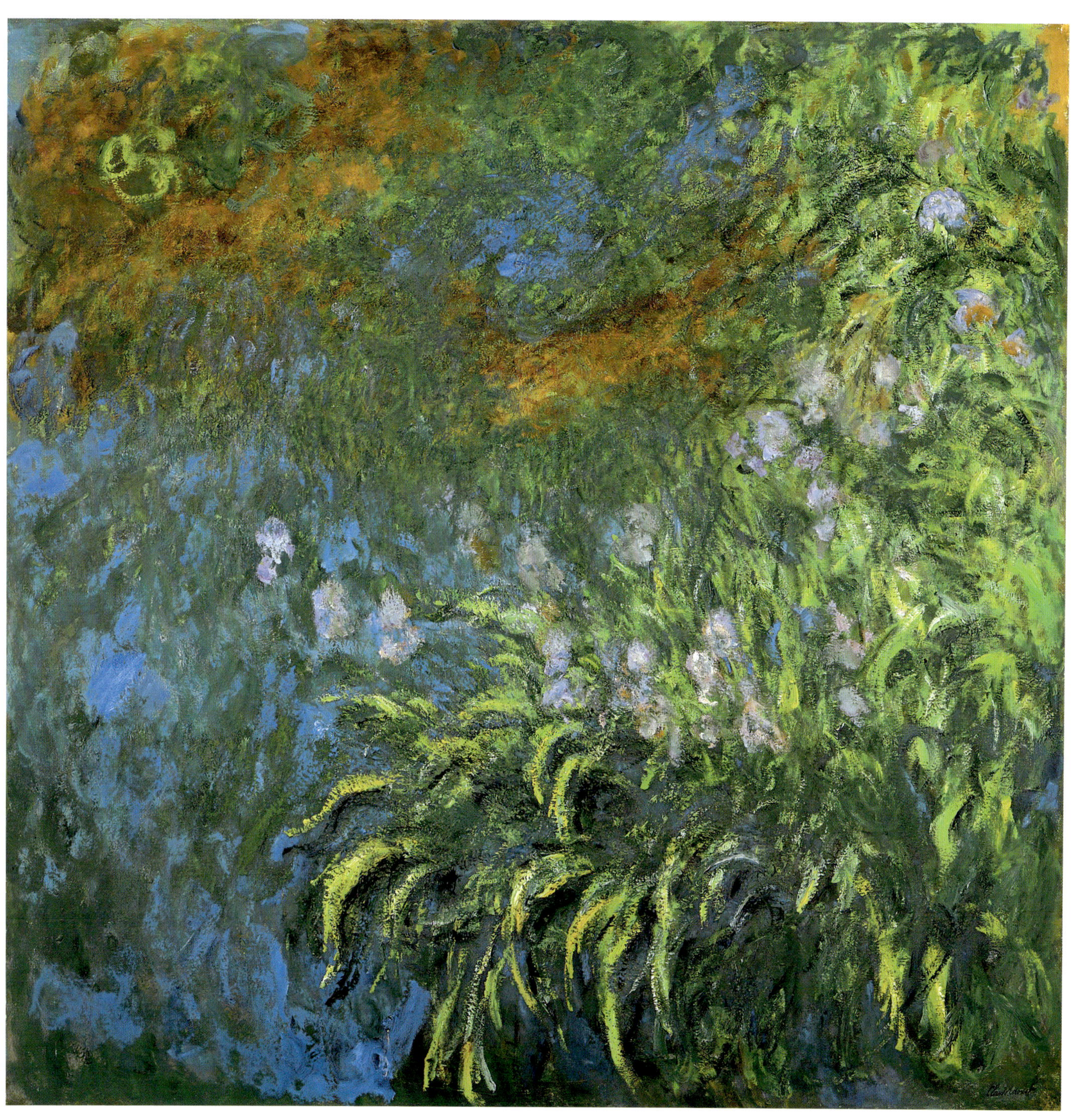

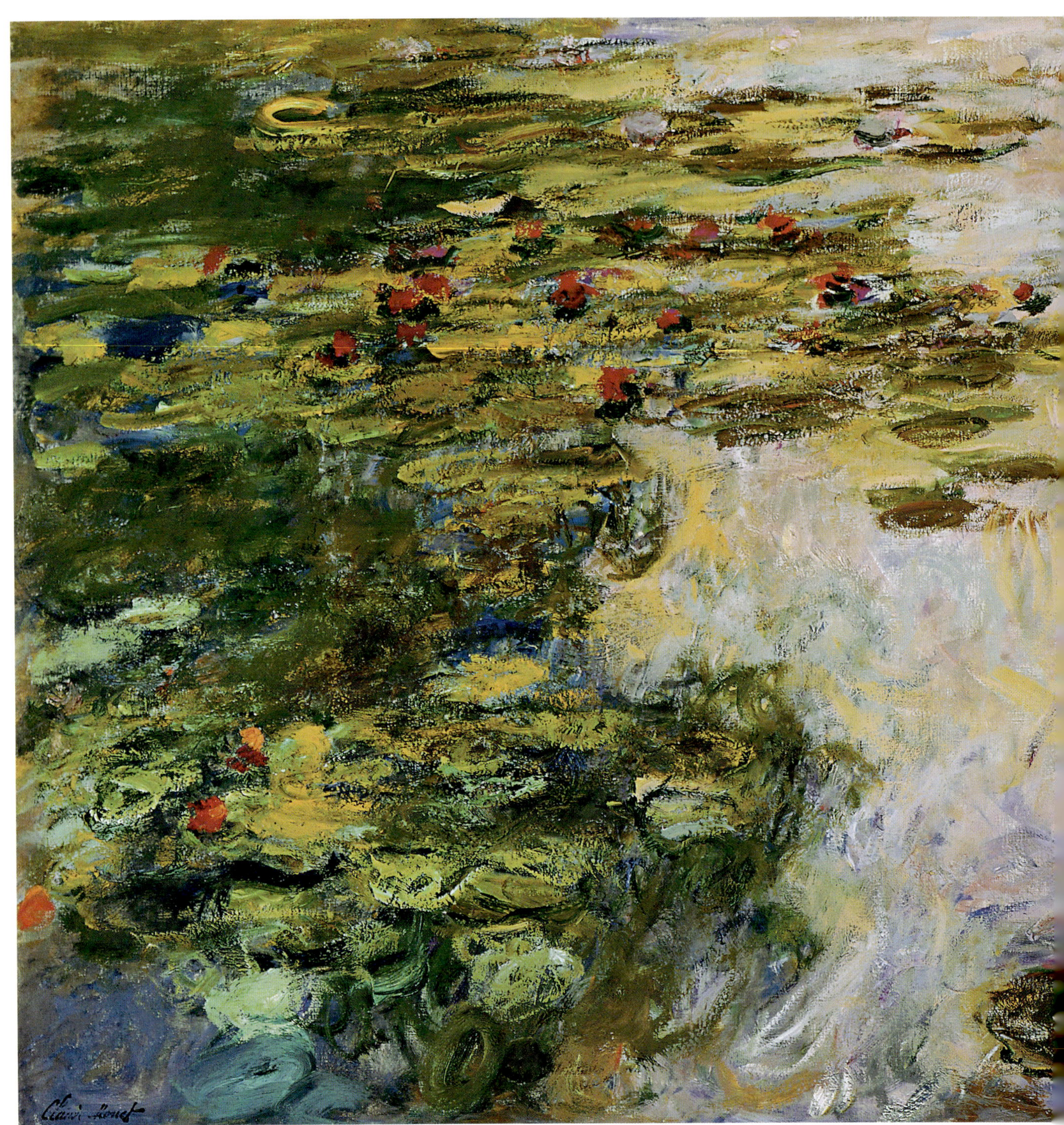

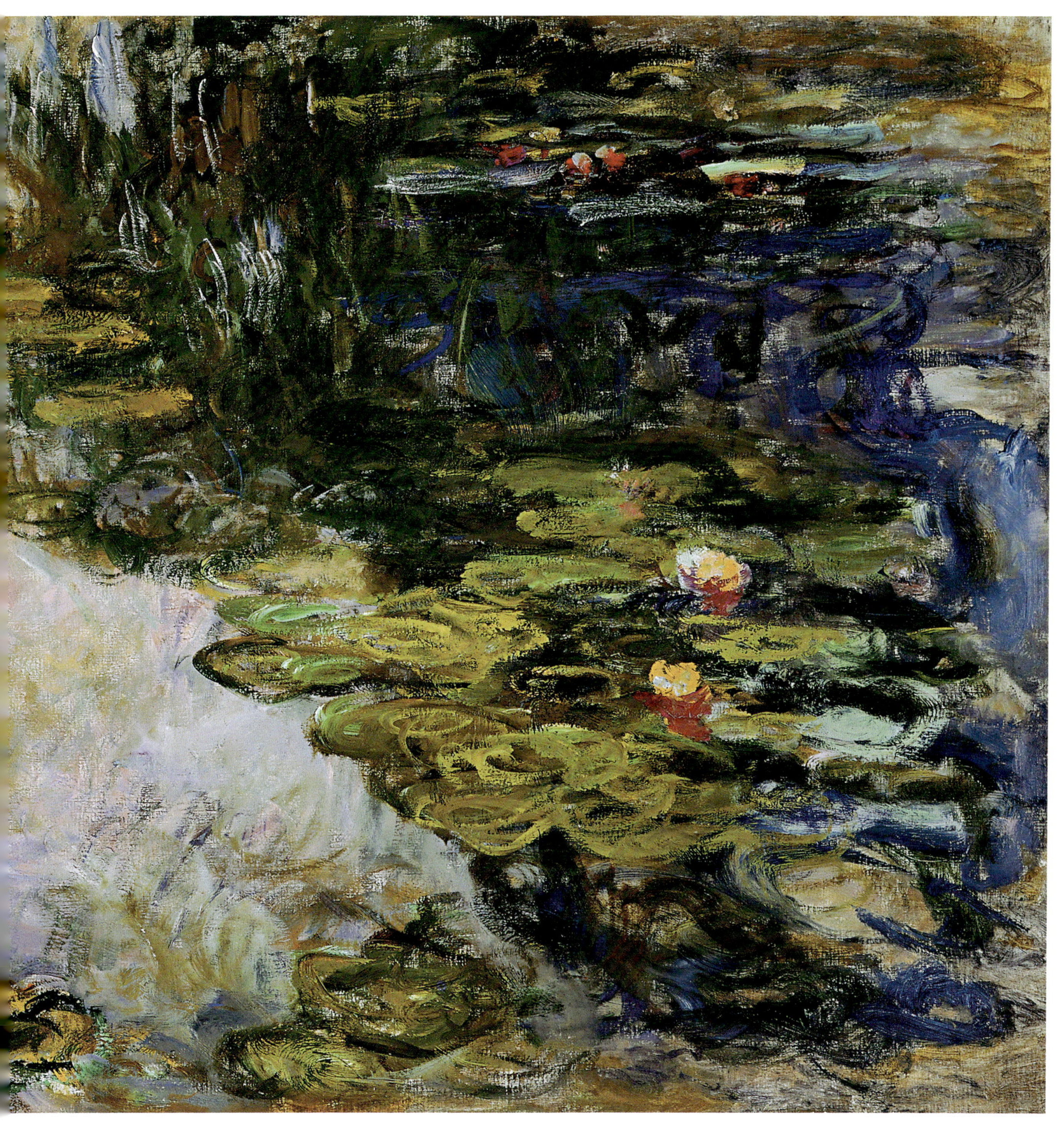

(right) As they appear in his earliest garden paintings, it seems safe to assume that roses were Monet's first love. In his own gardens, climbers obediently scaled the frames built for them, or scrambled up tree trunks; festooned arches, or ascended tripod-like *tuteurs;* and clung to the walls of the pink house. Shrub roses were allowed to grow naturally or were clipped and pruned into standards, which resembled small trees.

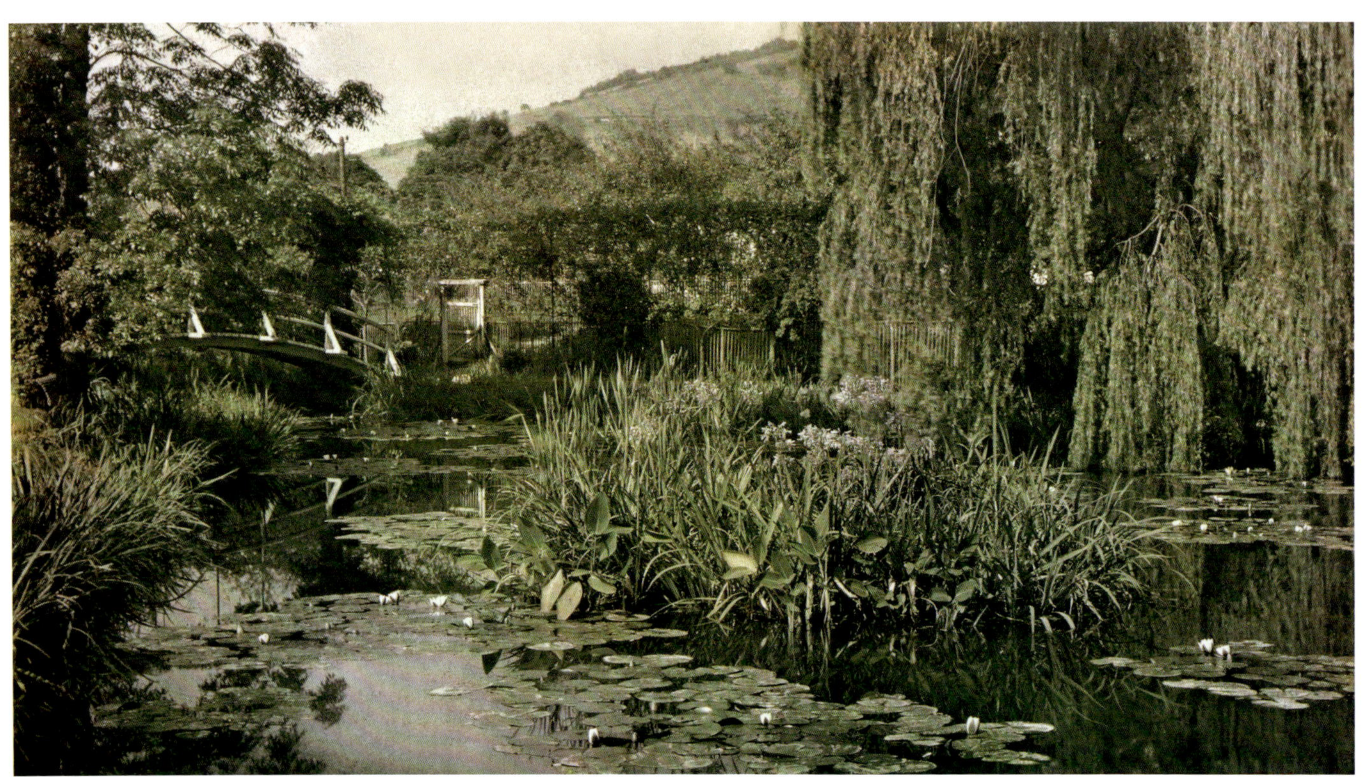

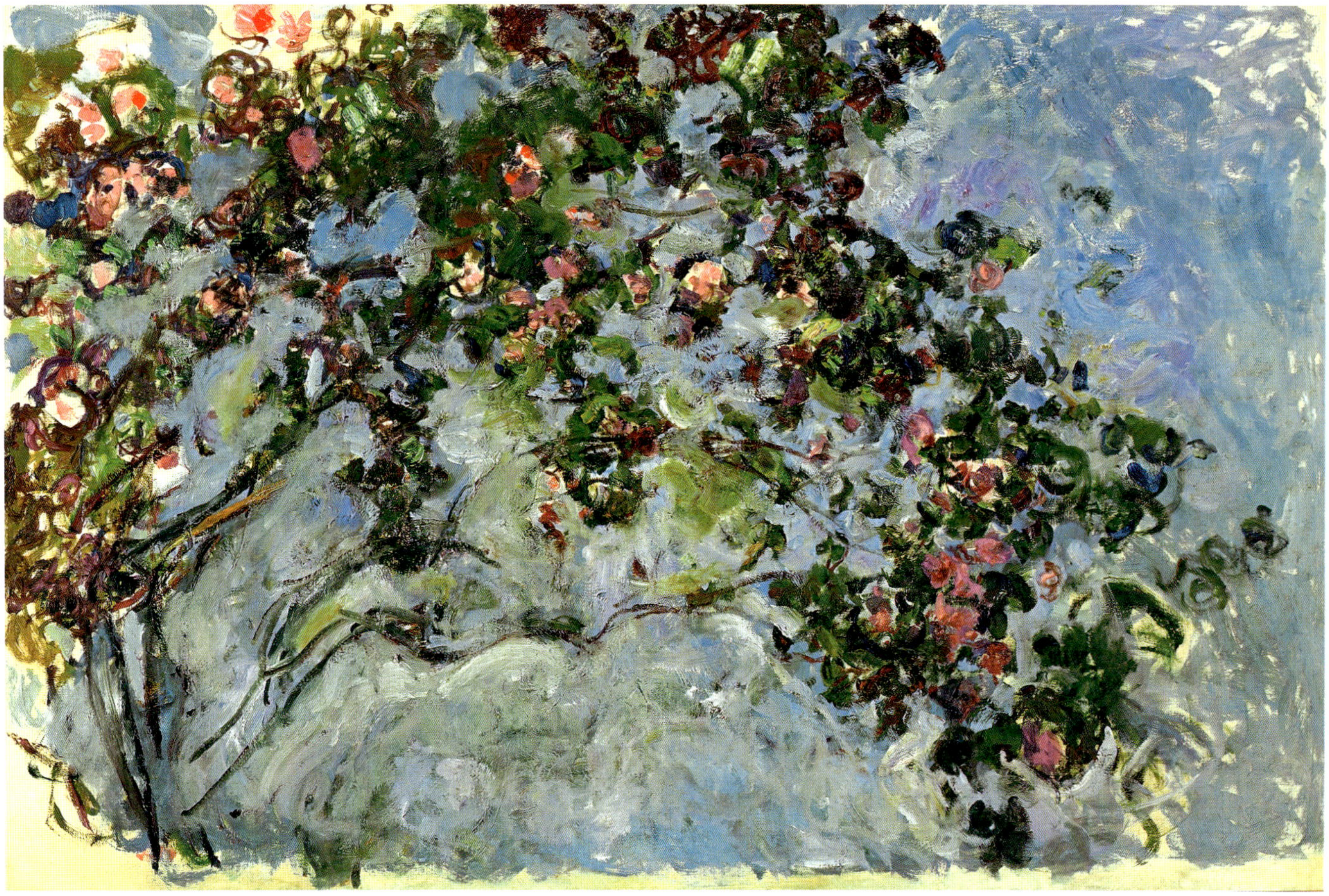

(following page) While daylilies appear in his paintings much less frequently than irises, roses, geraniums, and gladioli, Monet must have felt an affinity for their ephemeral blossoms. *Hemerocallis*, the daylily's botanical name, from Greek *hemera*, meaning "day," and *kallos*, "beauty," might be translated as "beautiful for a day." Each bloom lasts only twenty-four hours, and thus daylilies are the quintessential "impressionist" flowers.

(right) Of the herbaceous perennials, irises were always high on Monet's list of favorites, both the cultivated bearded varieties and the wild species like the yellow flag, which he grew in the water garden.

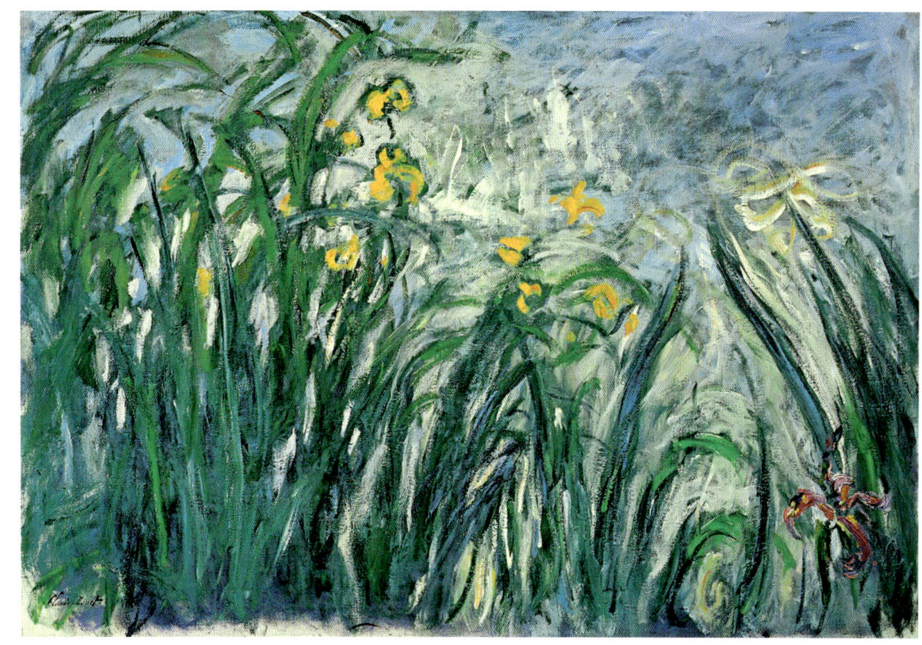

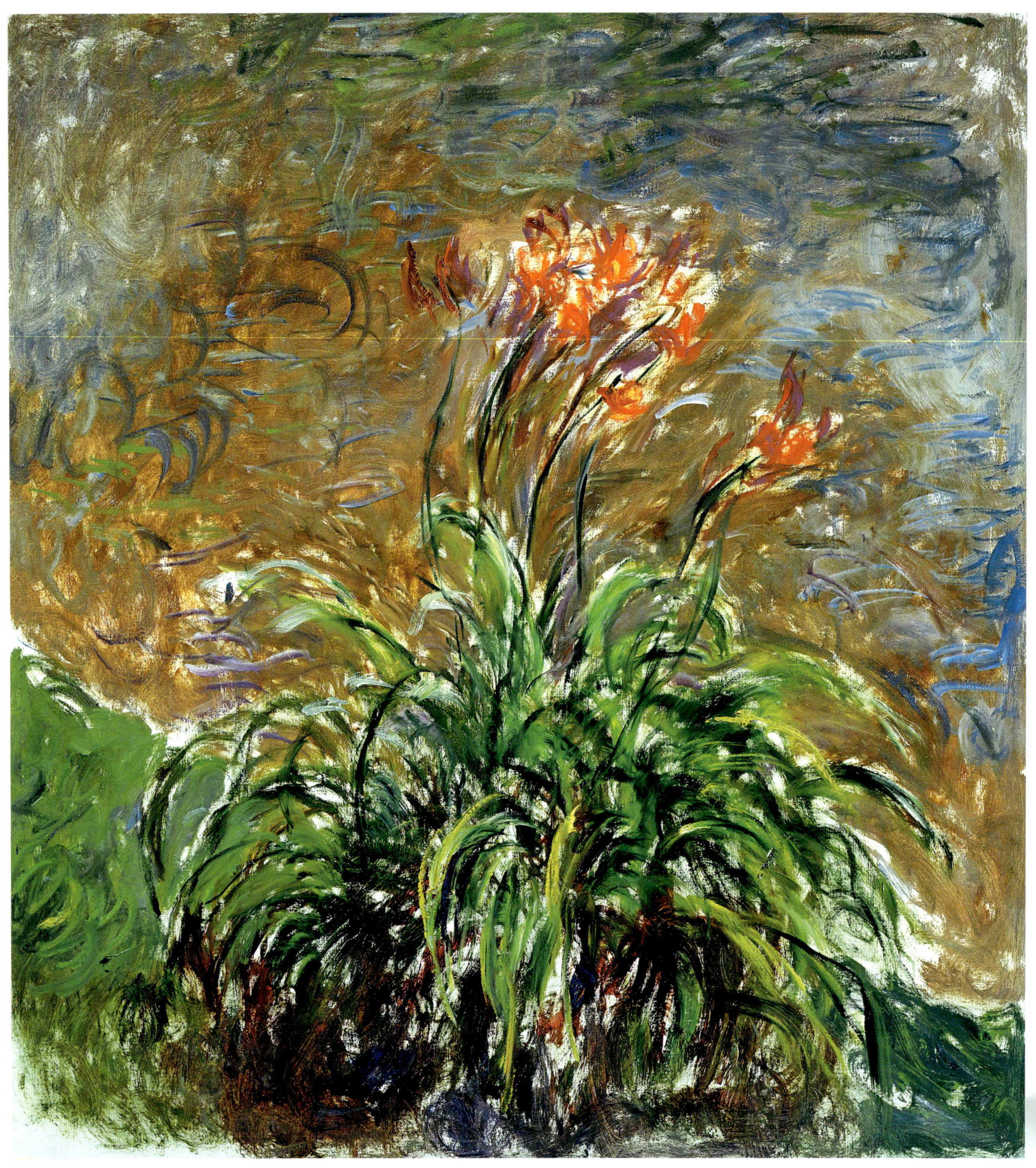

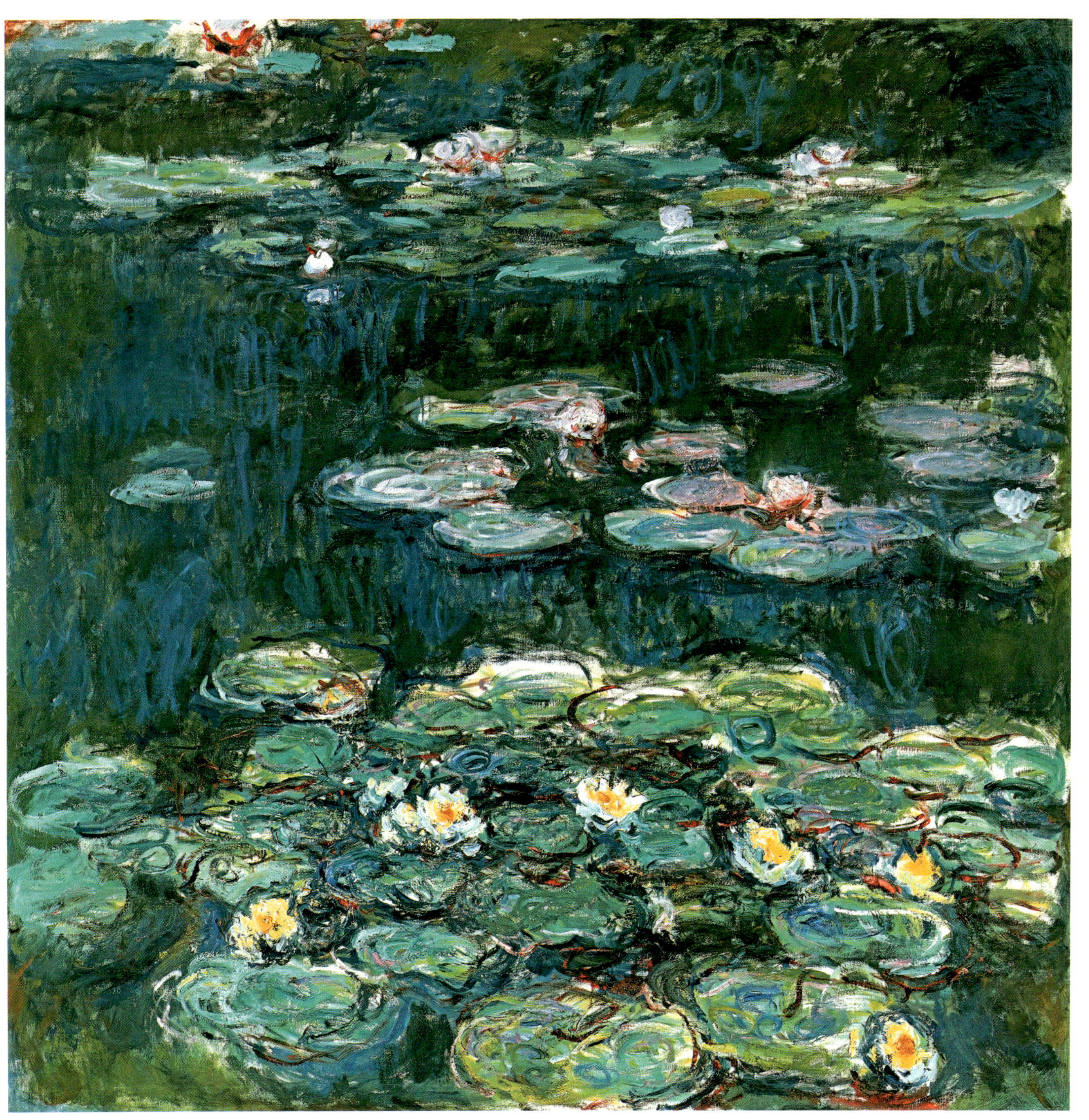

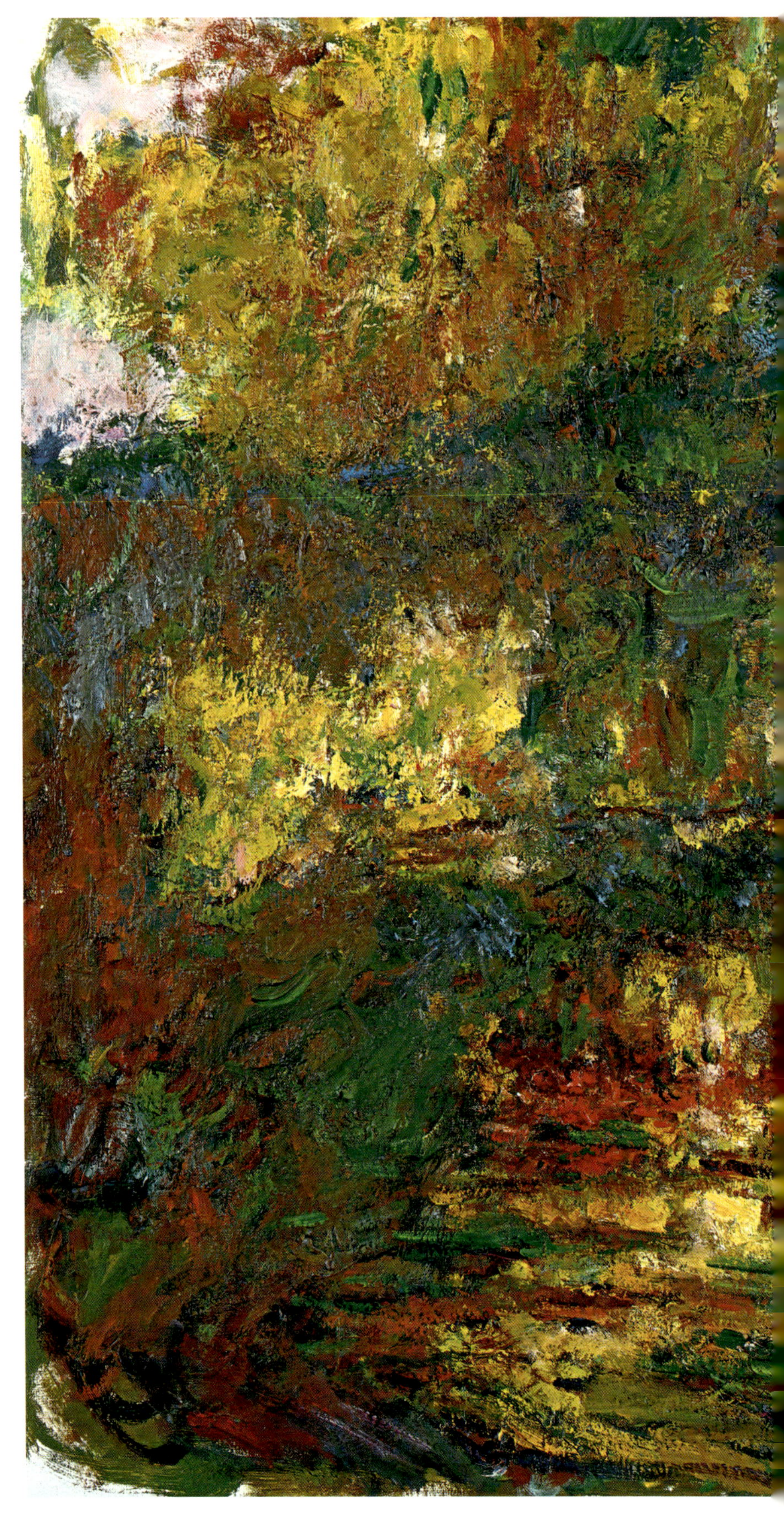

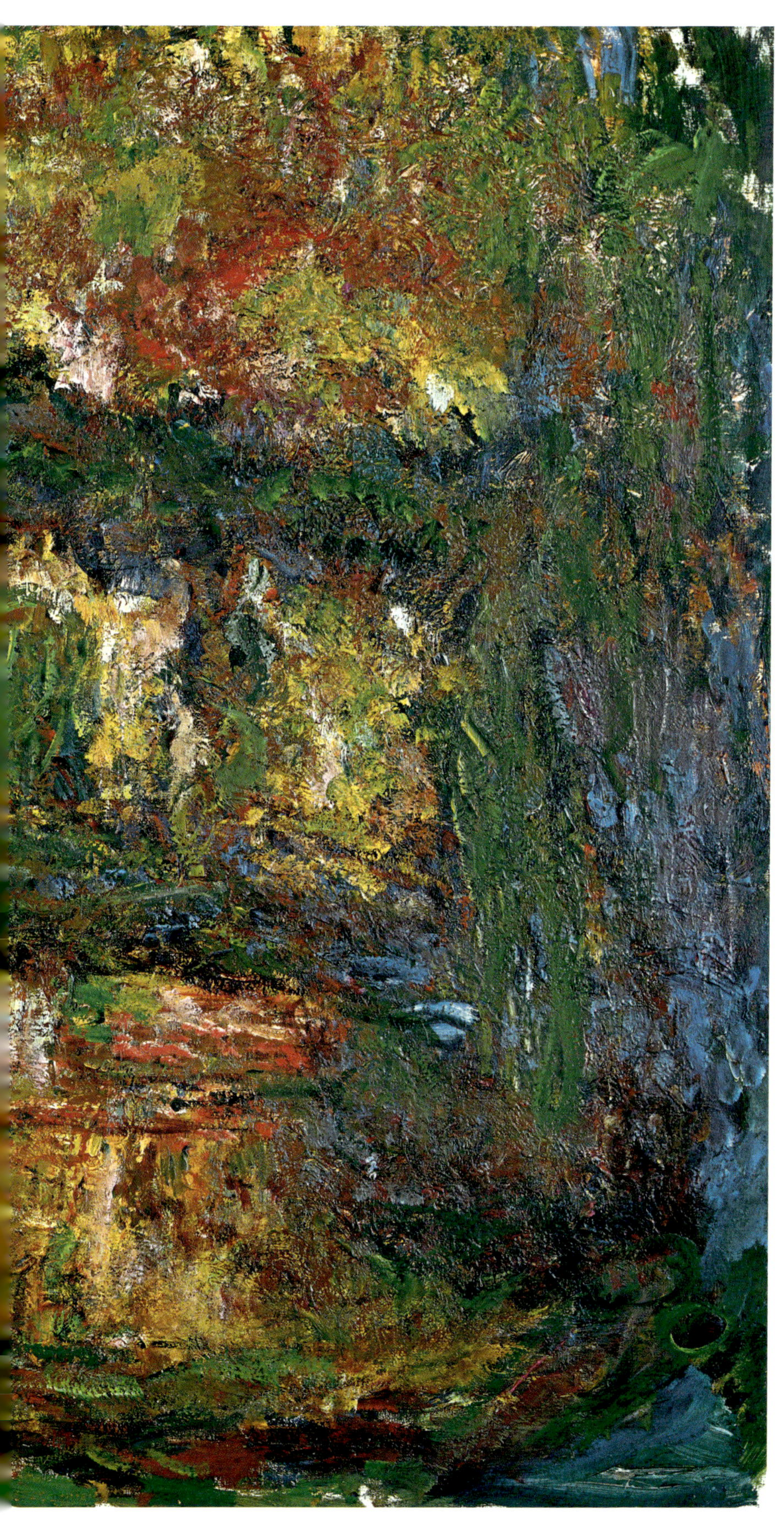

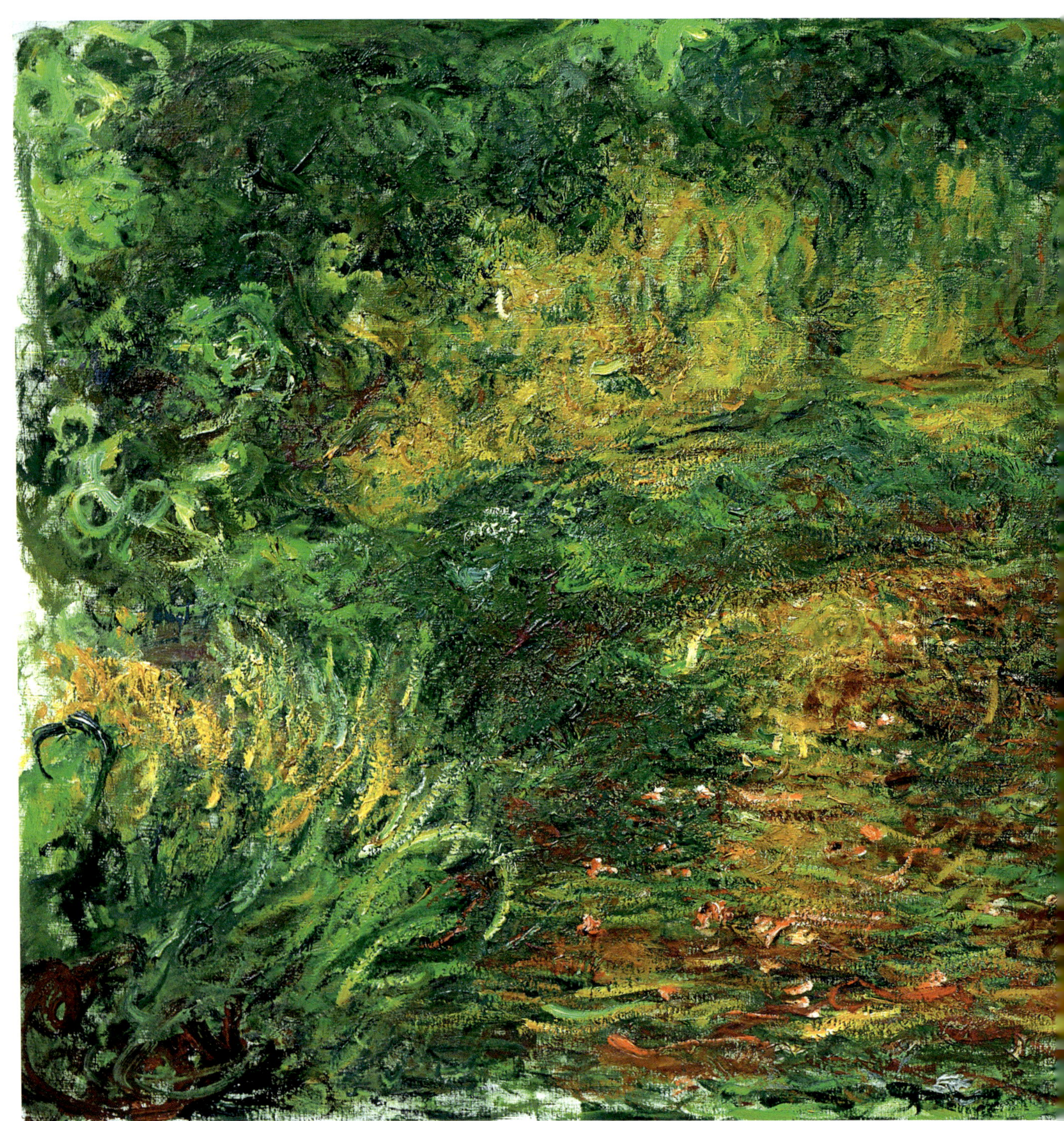

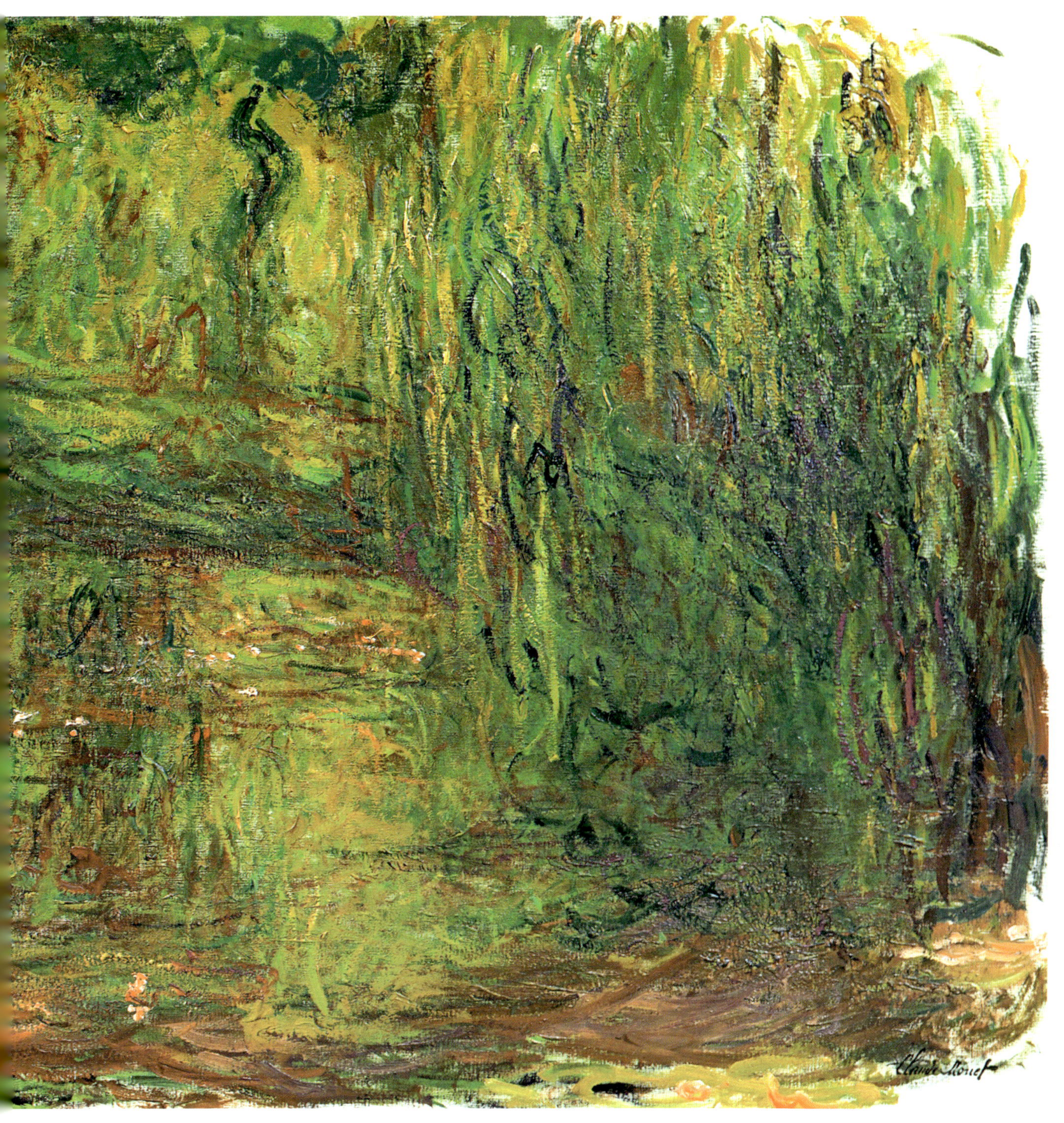
Claude Monet

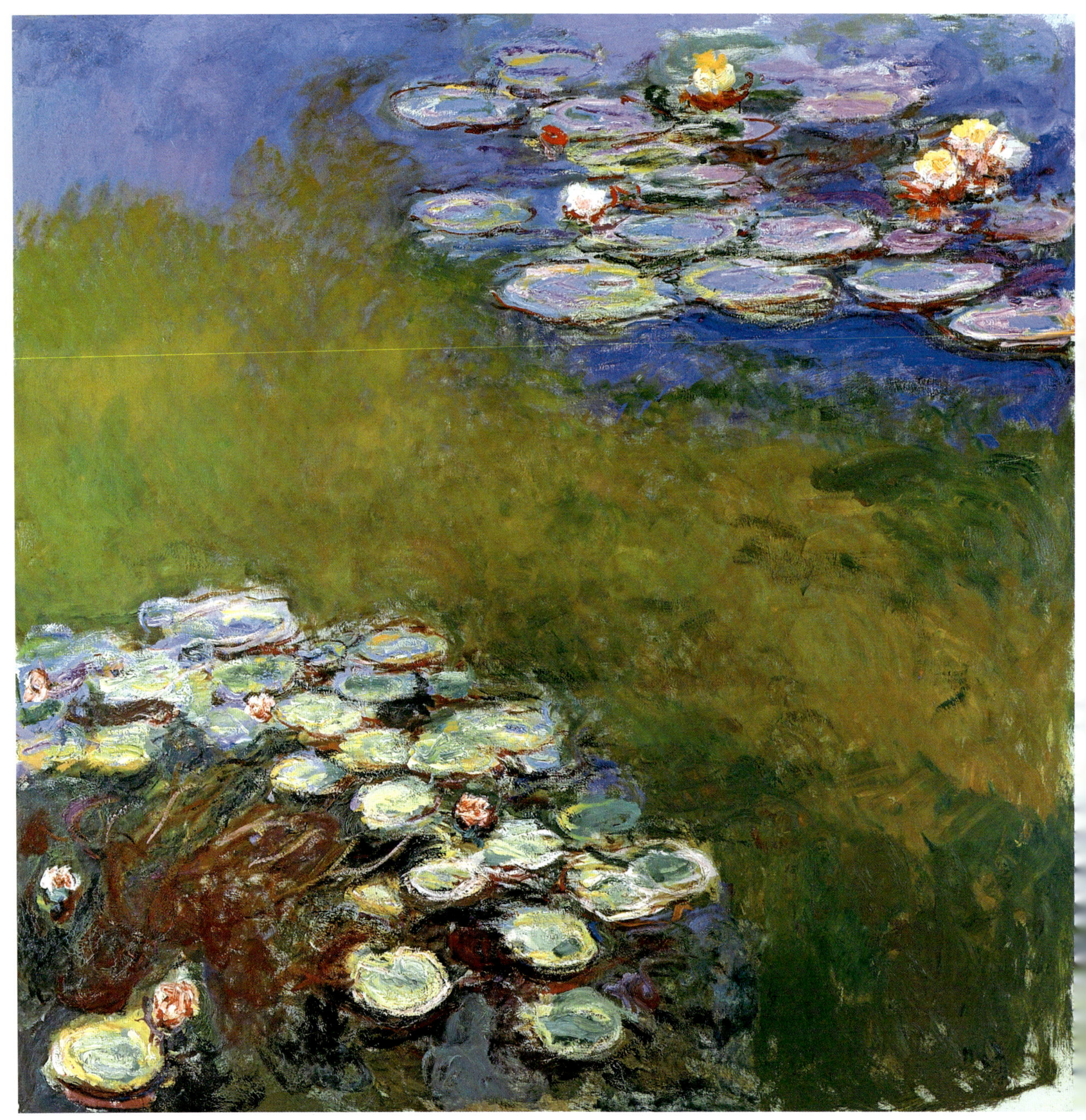

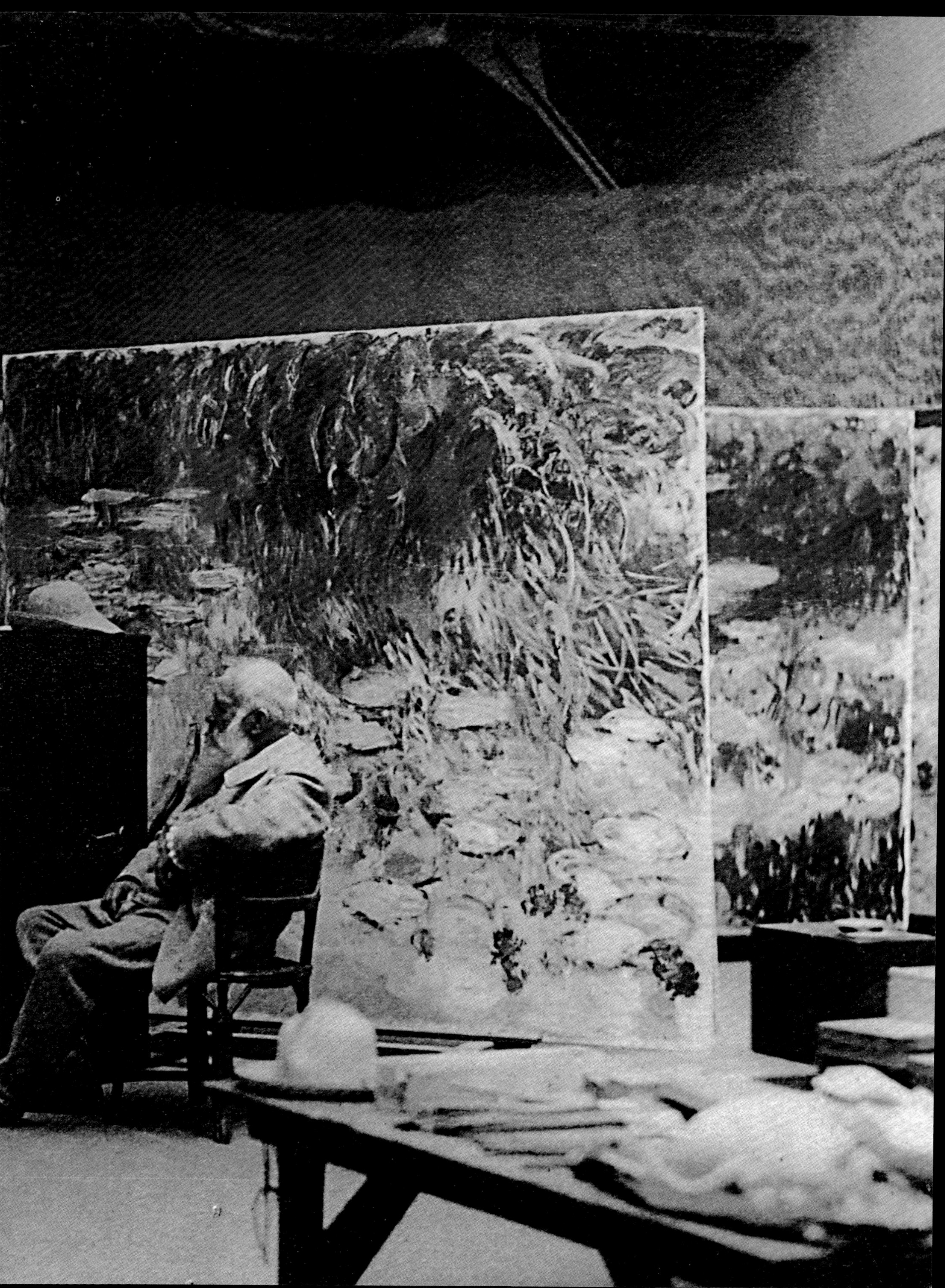

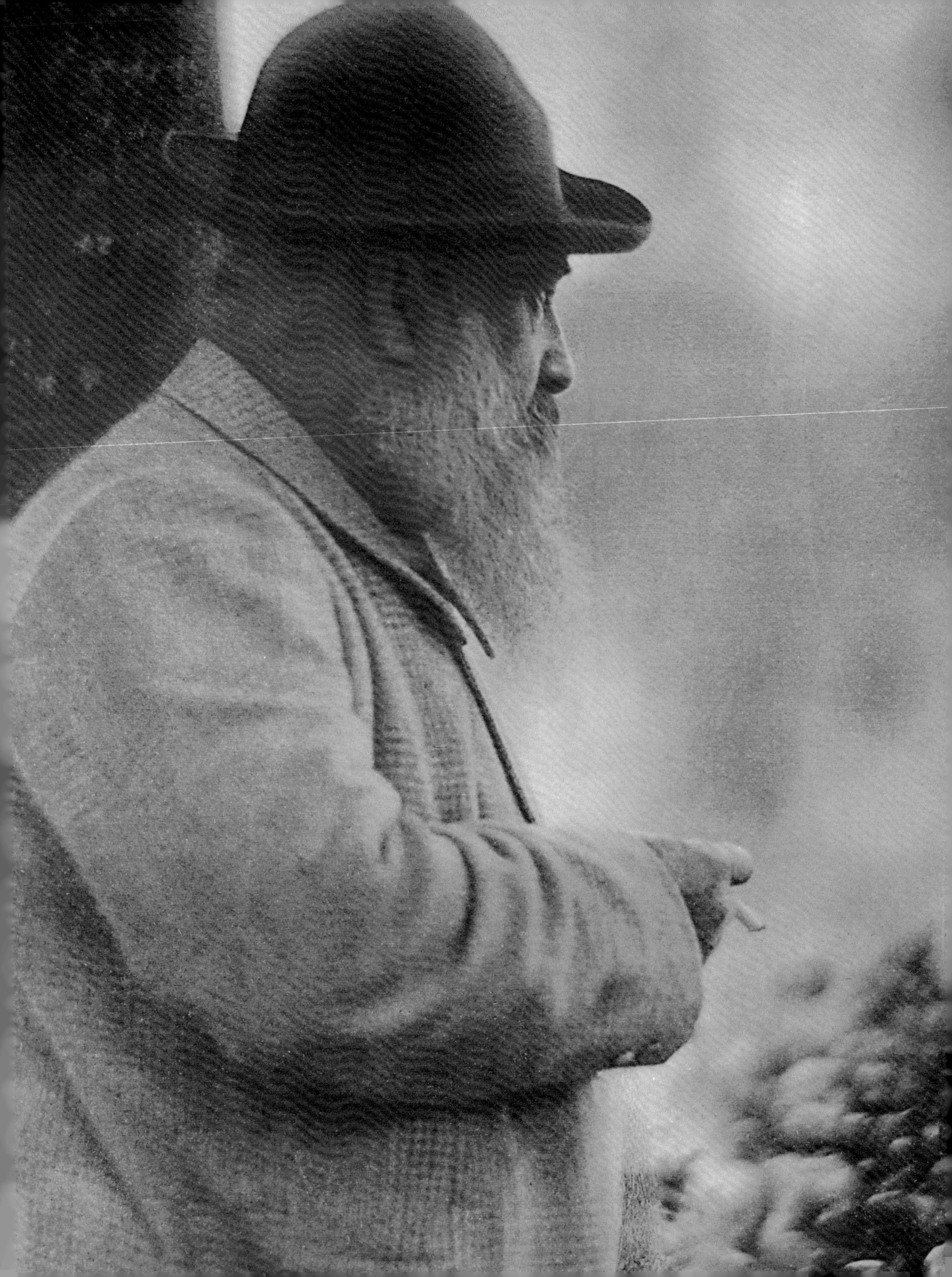

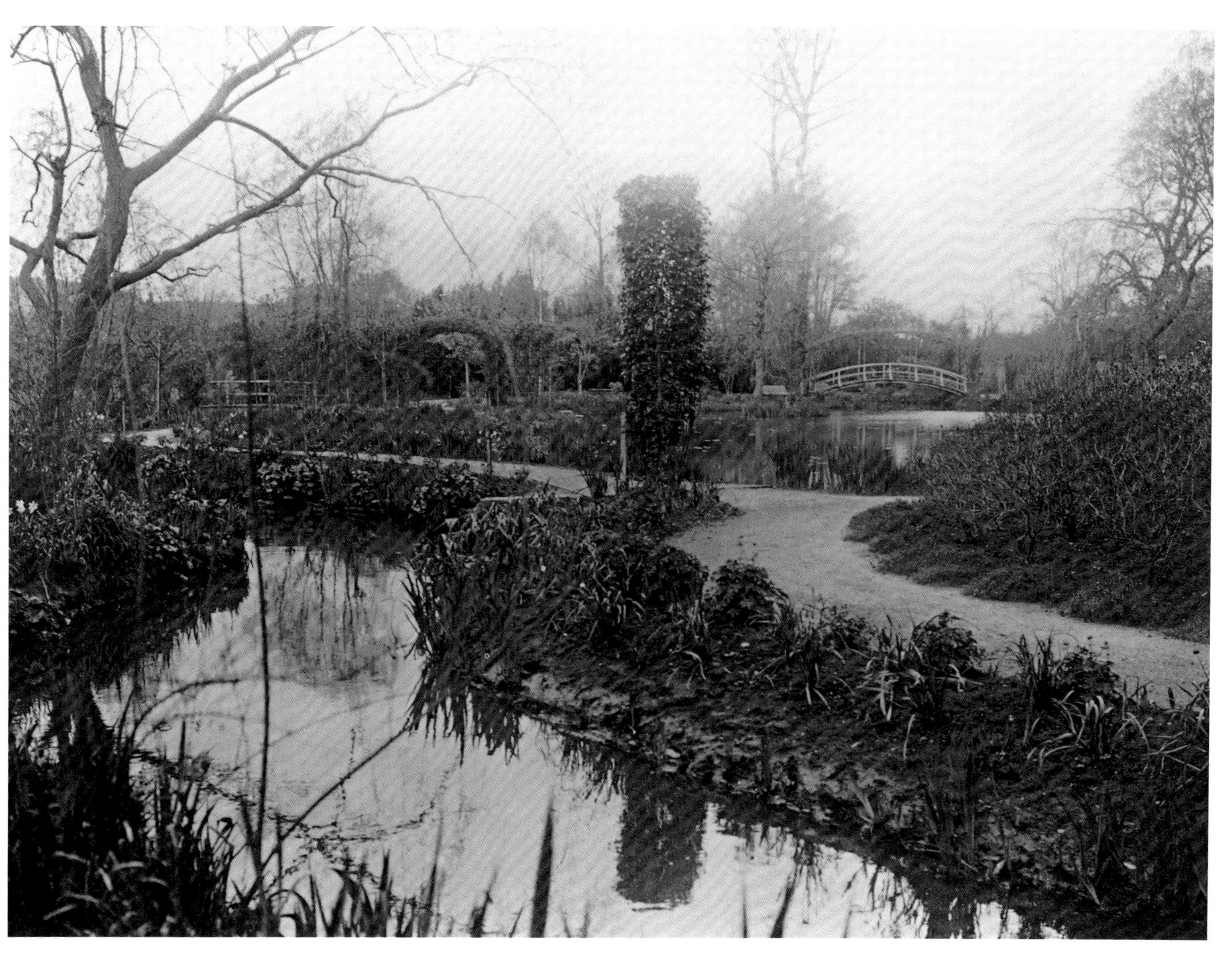

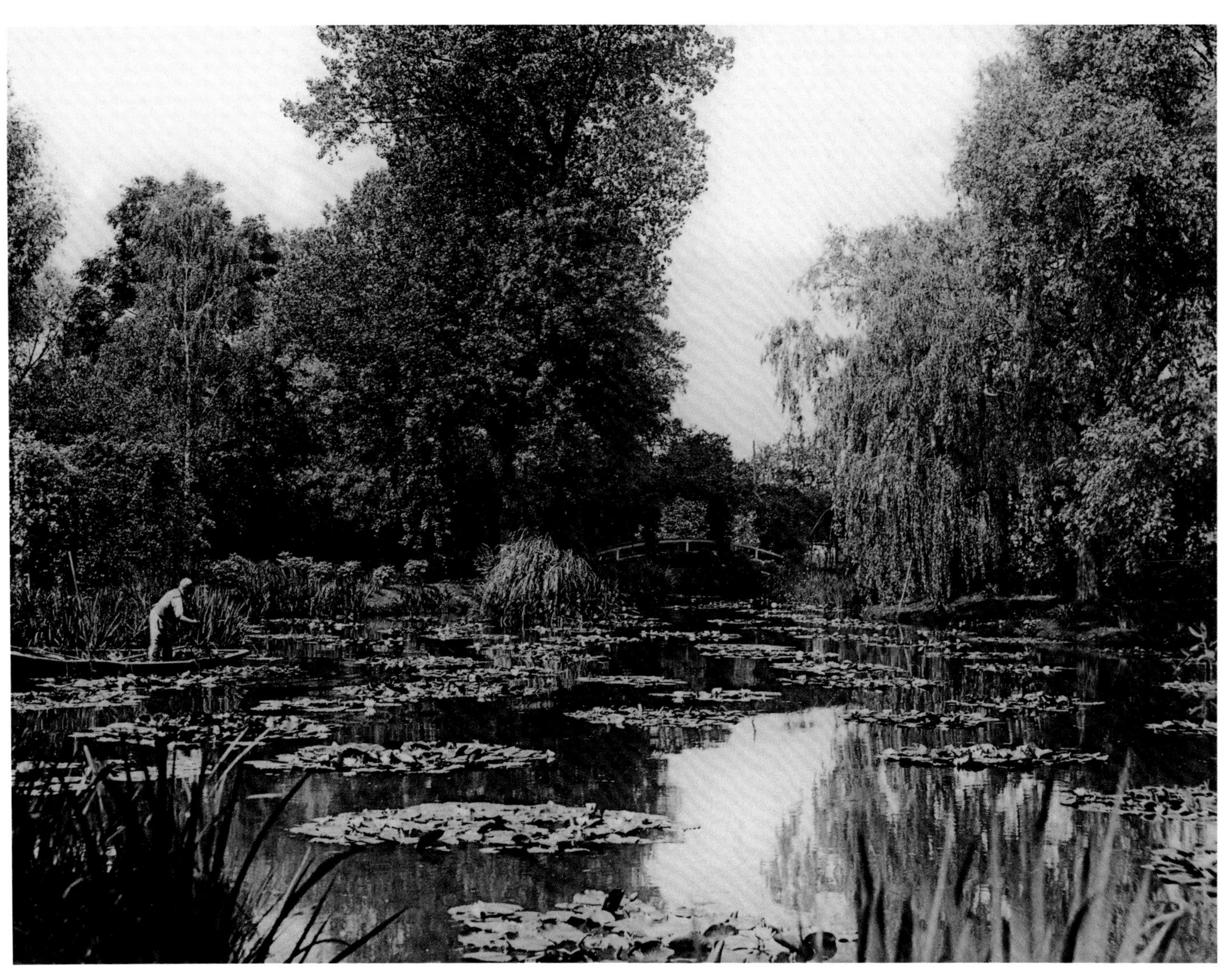

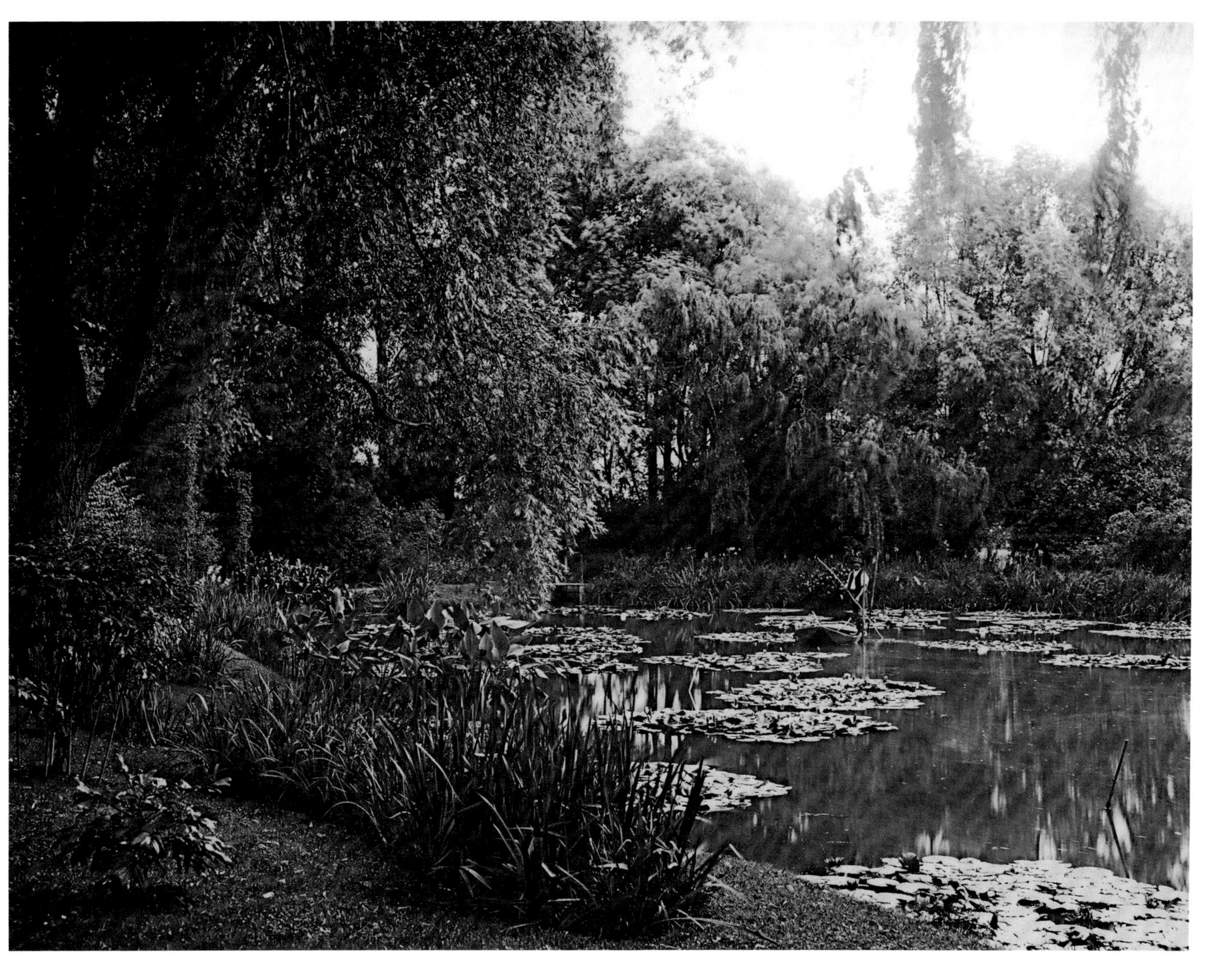

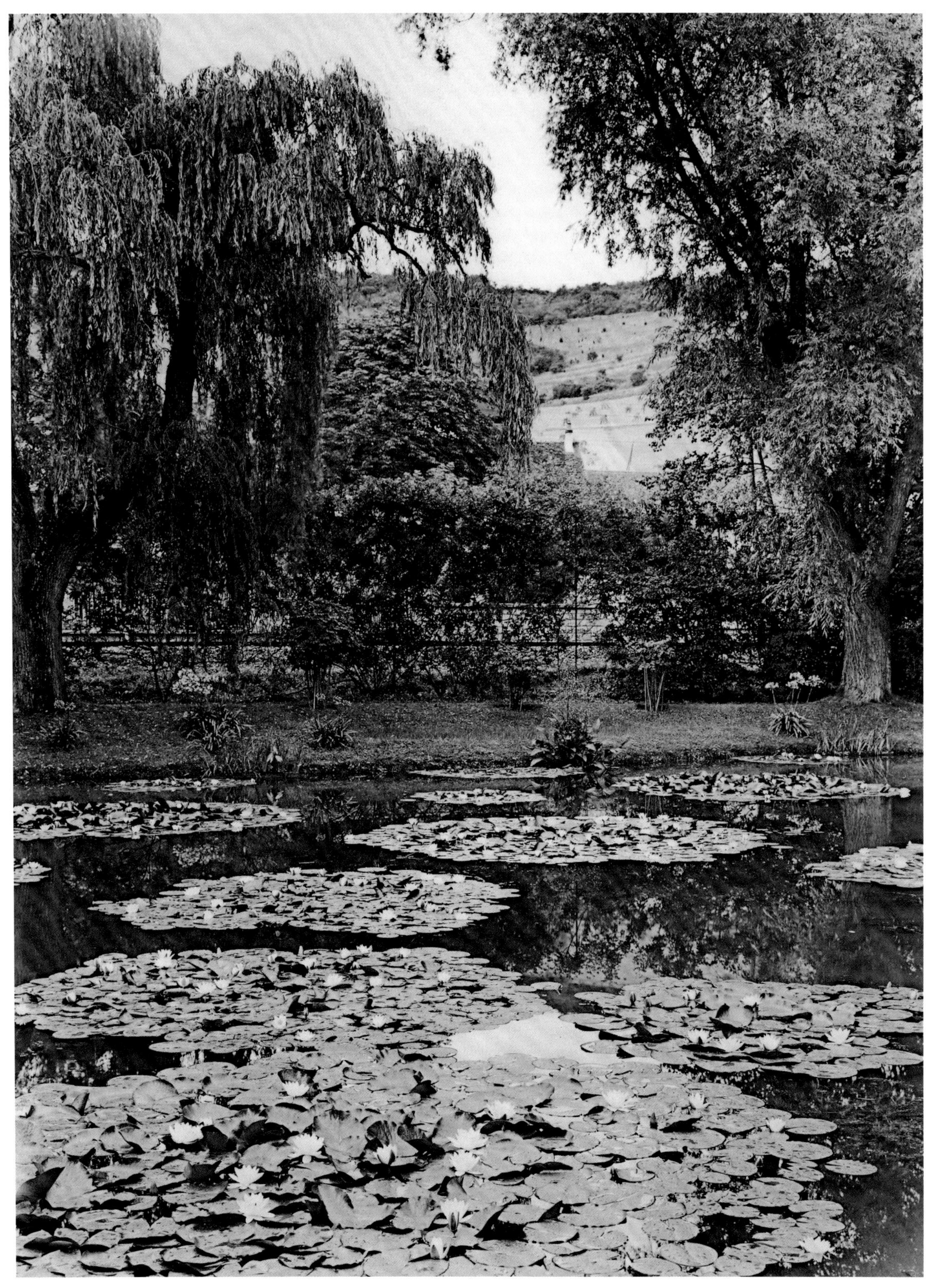

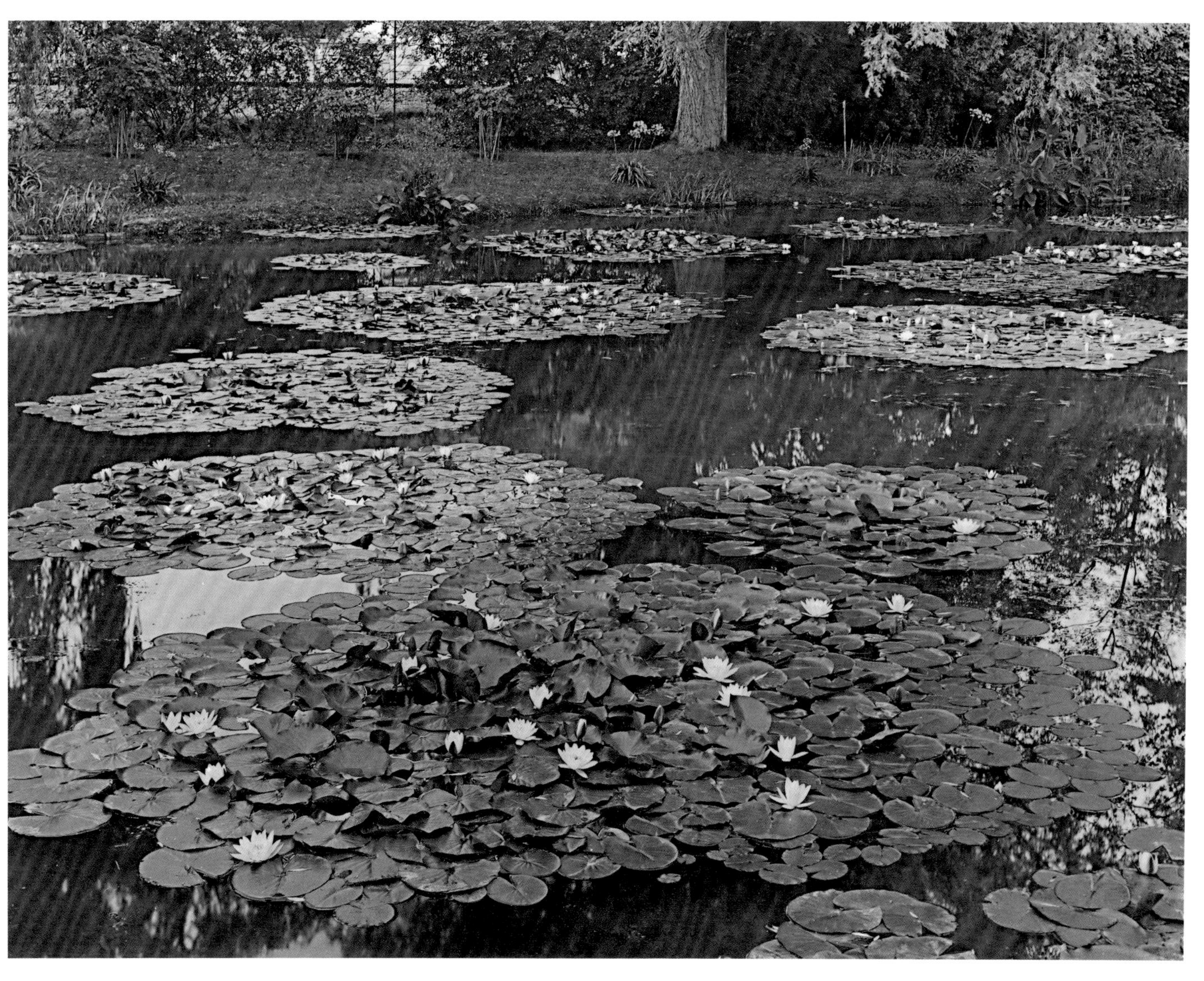

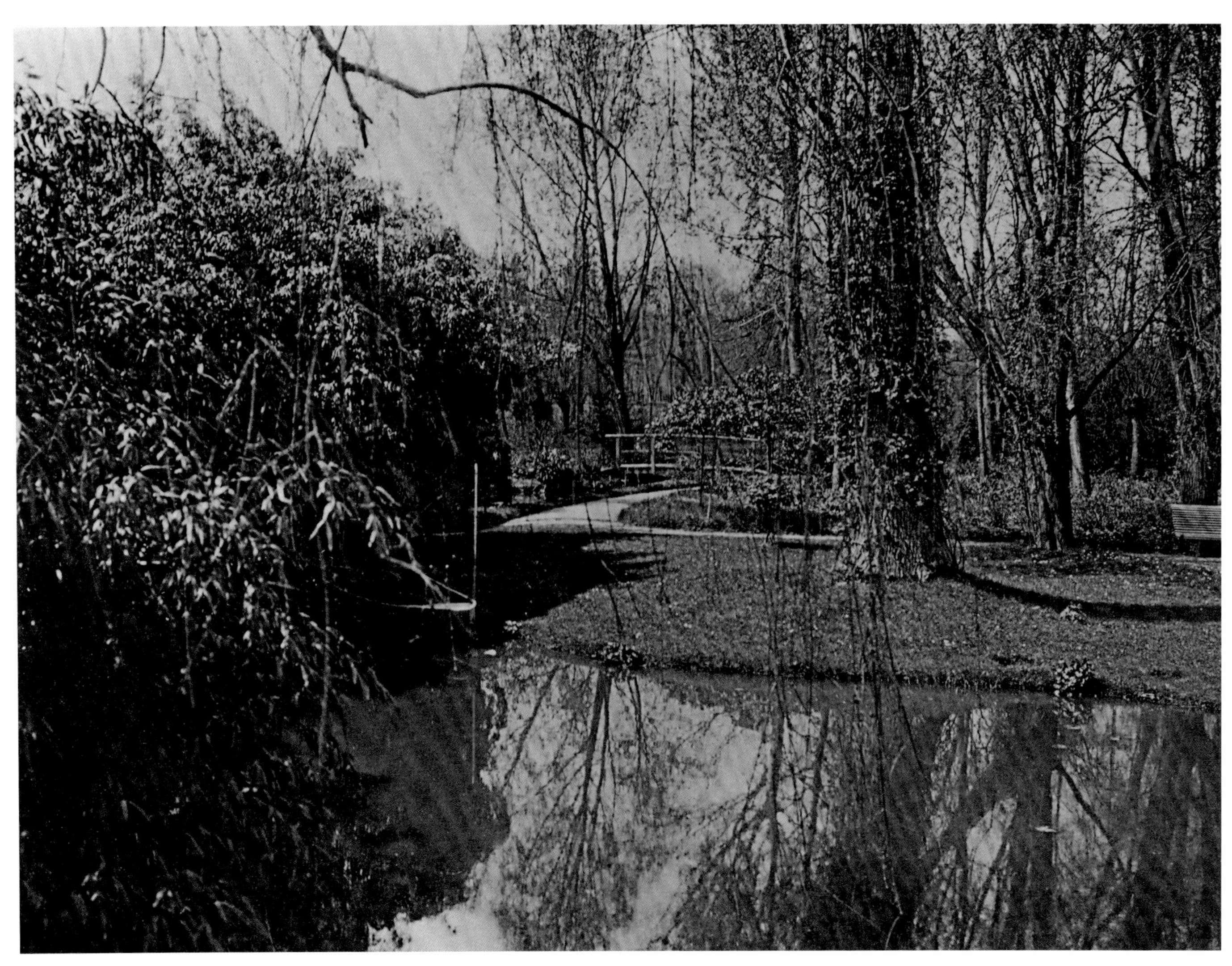

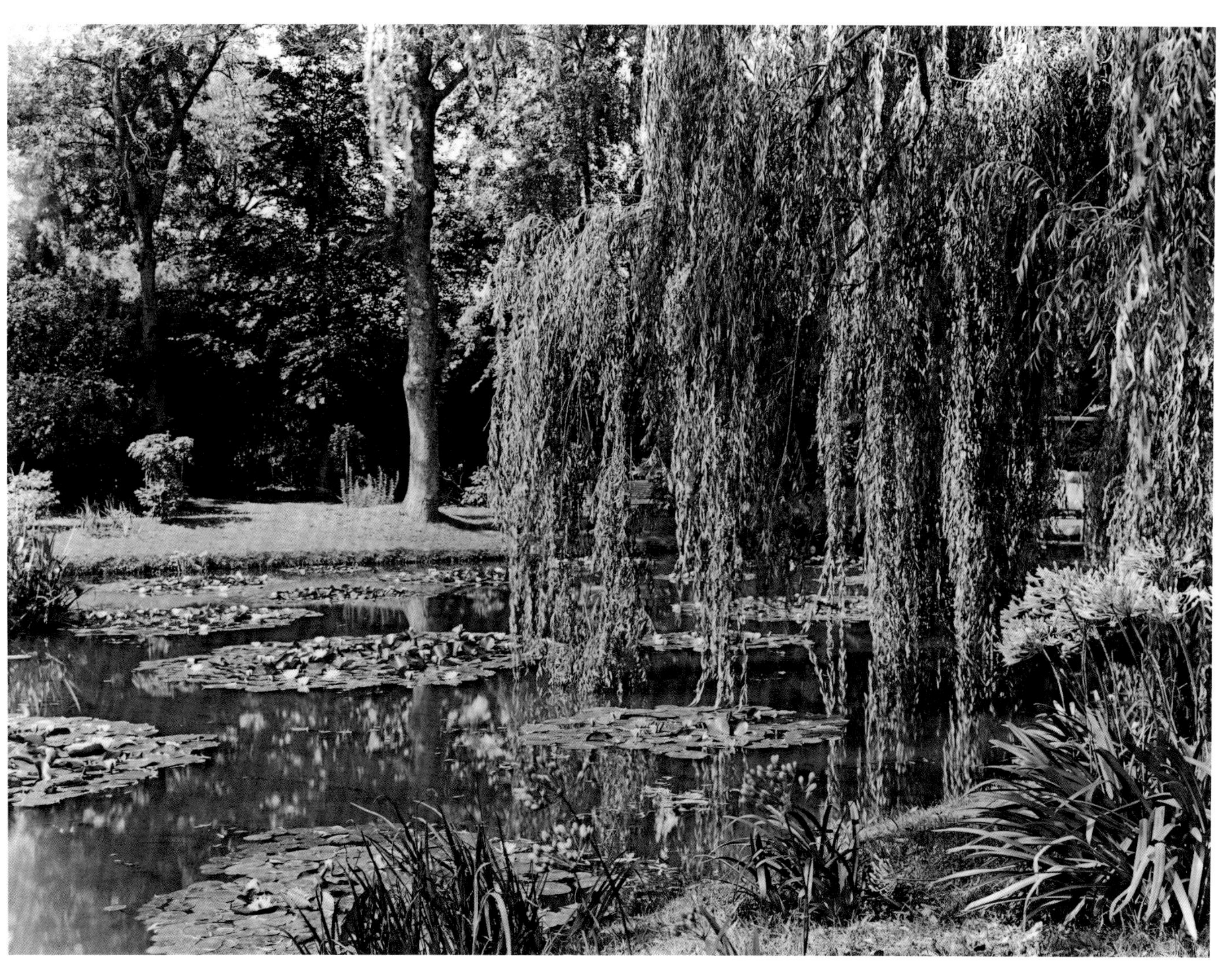

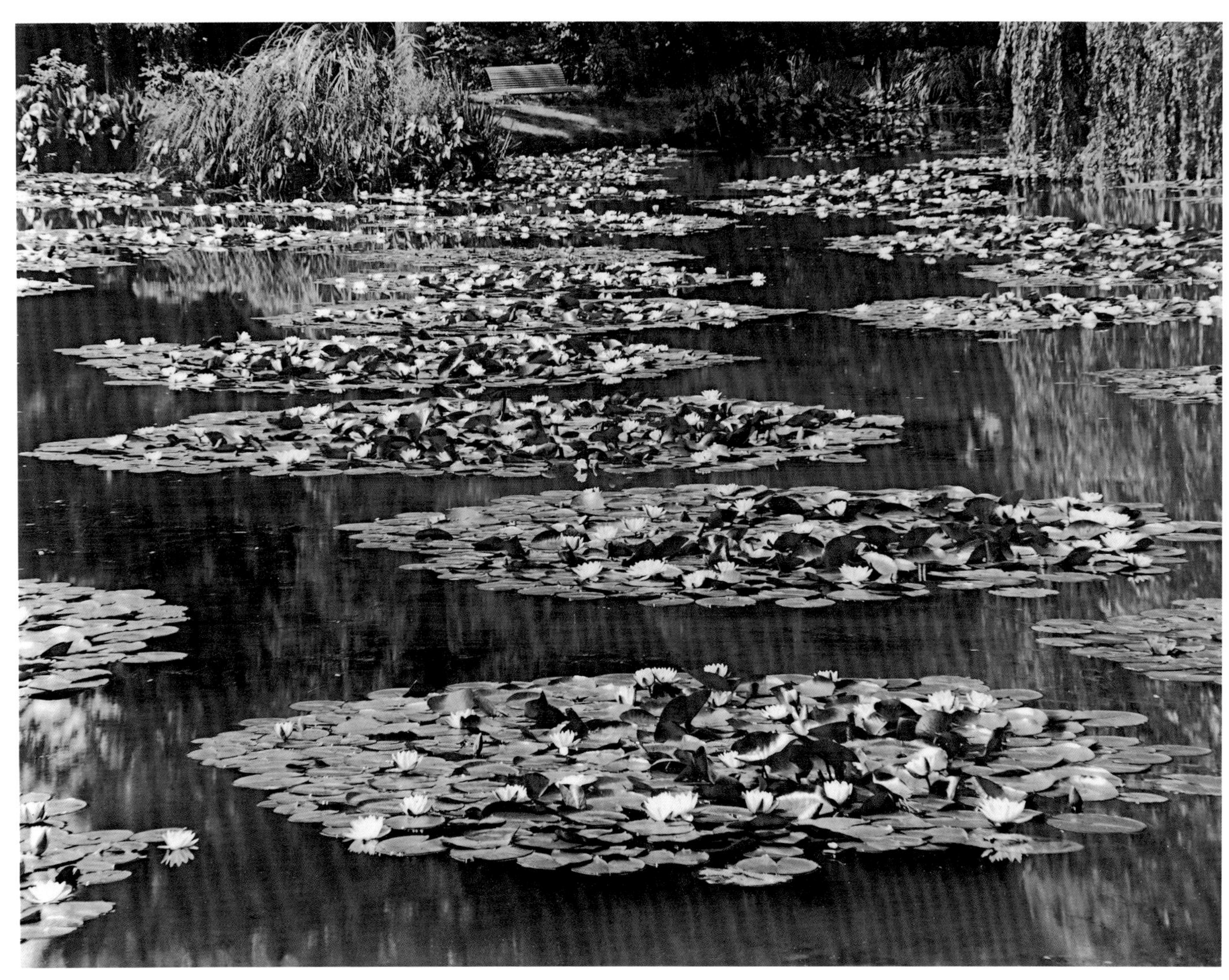

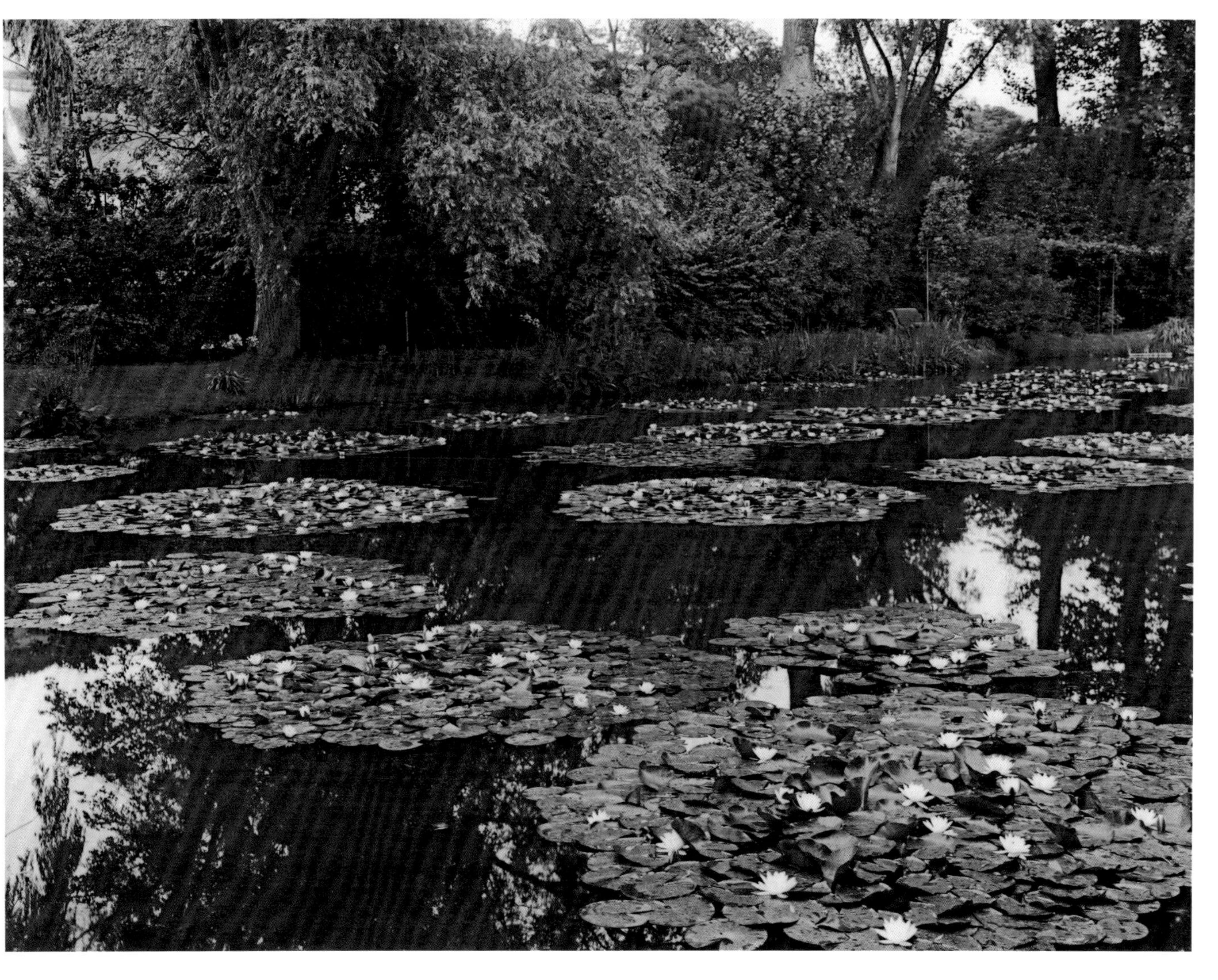

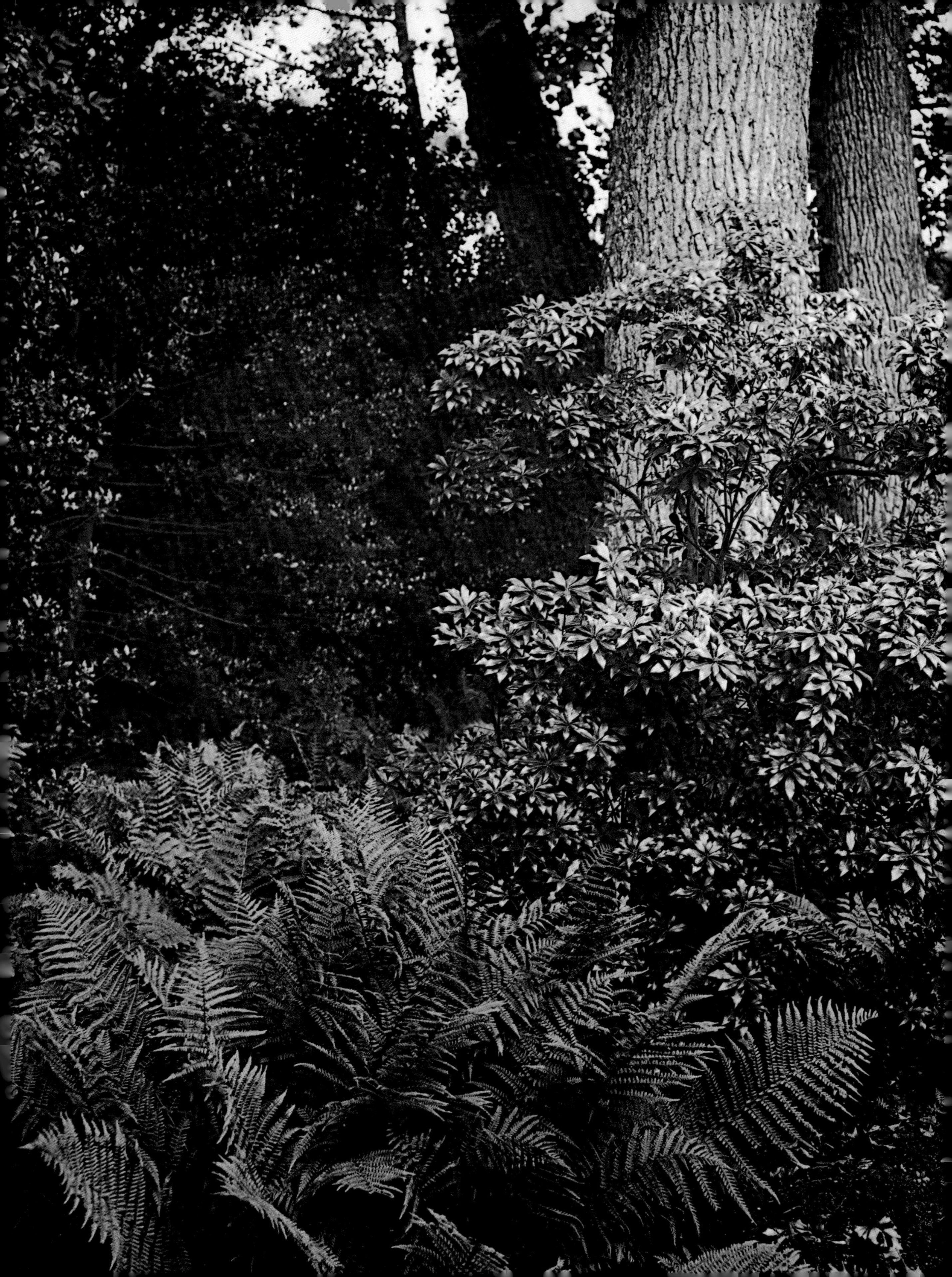

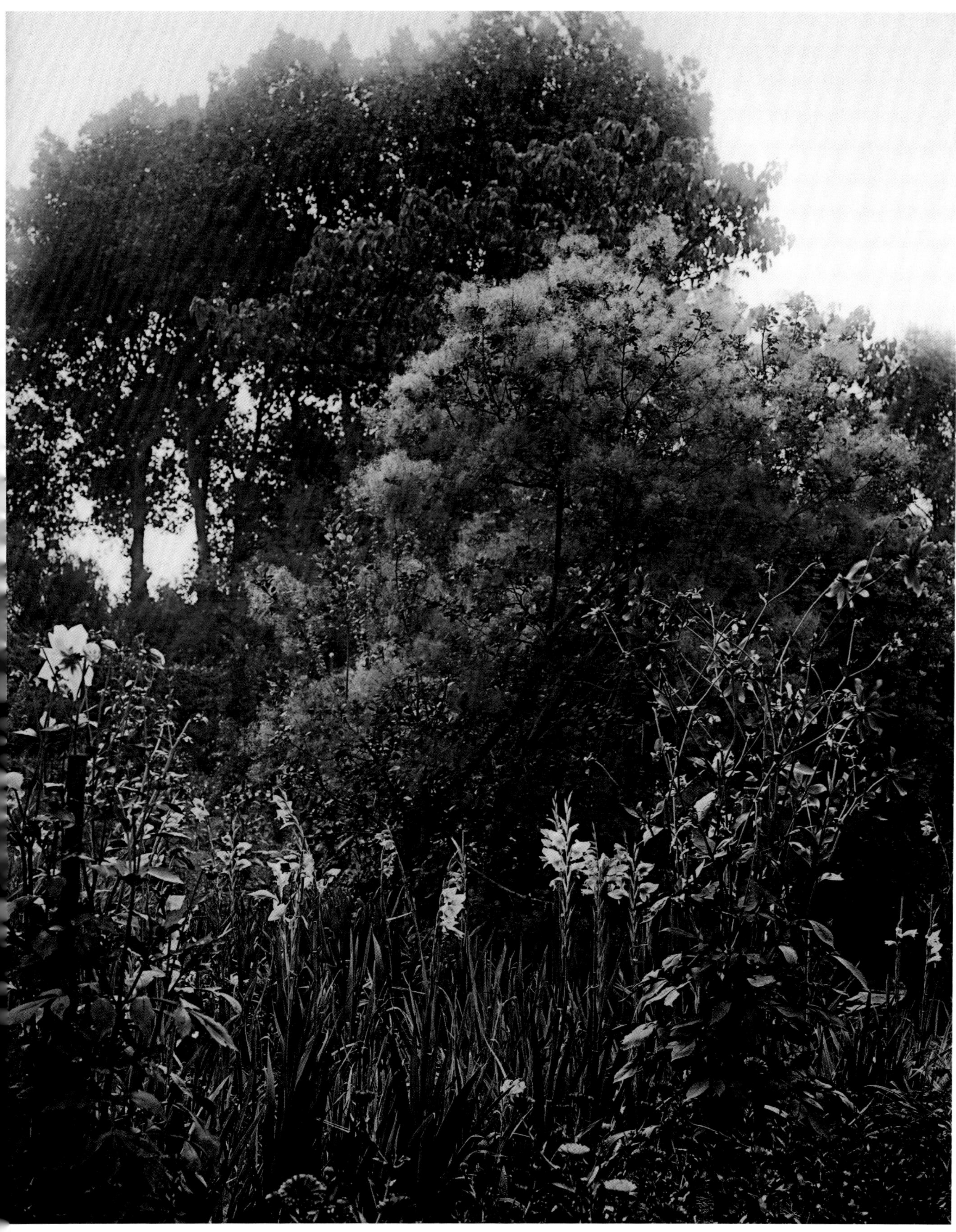

These two photographs dating from June 1921 were taken by Monsieur Kuroki, a relative of Kojiro Matsukata, one of the leading Japanese collectors of Impressionist paintings. Monet is surrounded by family members: Blanche Hoschedé-Monet, who devoted herself to his care after the death of her mother, Alice, in 1911; Michel, the painter's only surviving son; and Alice Butler, the daughter of Monet's favorite model, his stepdaughter Suzanne, whose death at a tender age was a terrible shock to Monet's wife. On the right stands Georges Clemenceau, one of the most charismatic characters of his age, who had recently lost the presidential election, after having guided his country to victory in World War I. He was the liaison among Monet, his friends, and the government, and would frequently visit Giverny to shake Monet out of moments of depression, caused by difficulties with his painting, anguish over the gardens, his diminishing eyesight due to cataracts, and his advanced age and ill health.

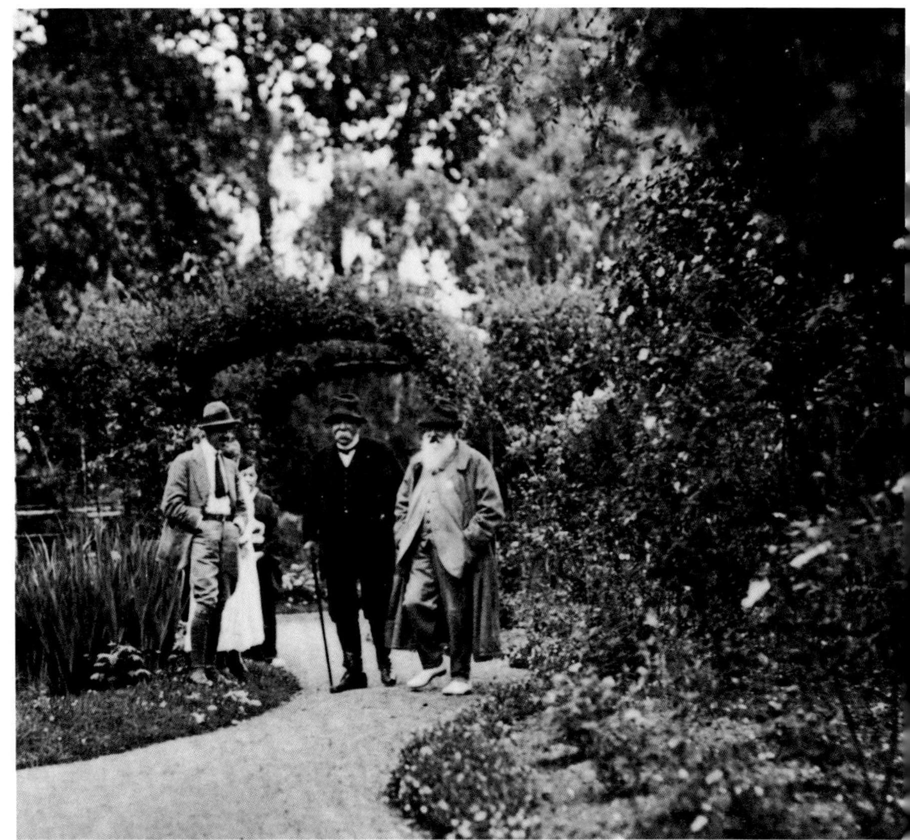

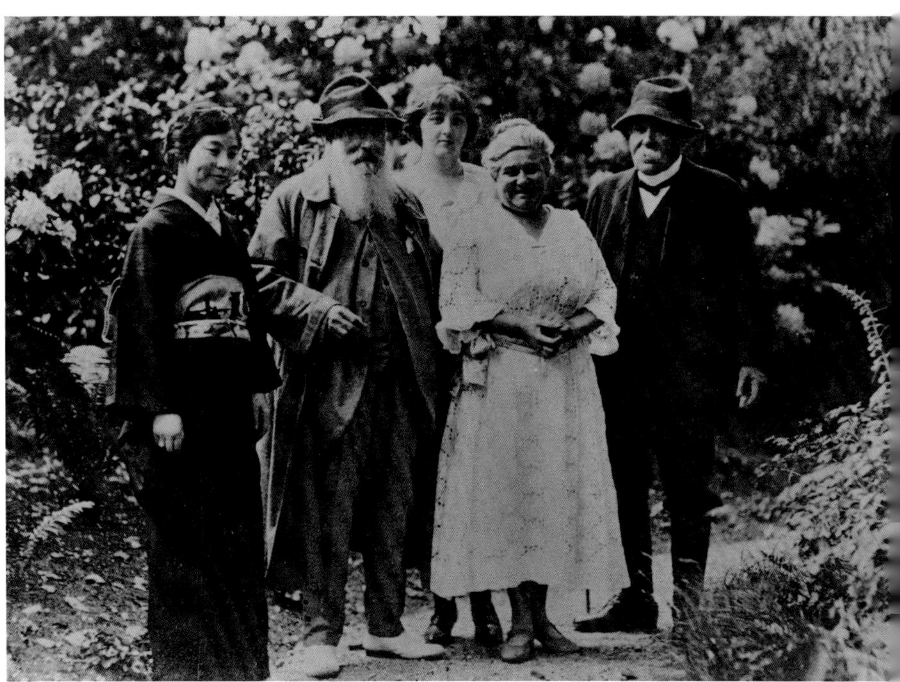

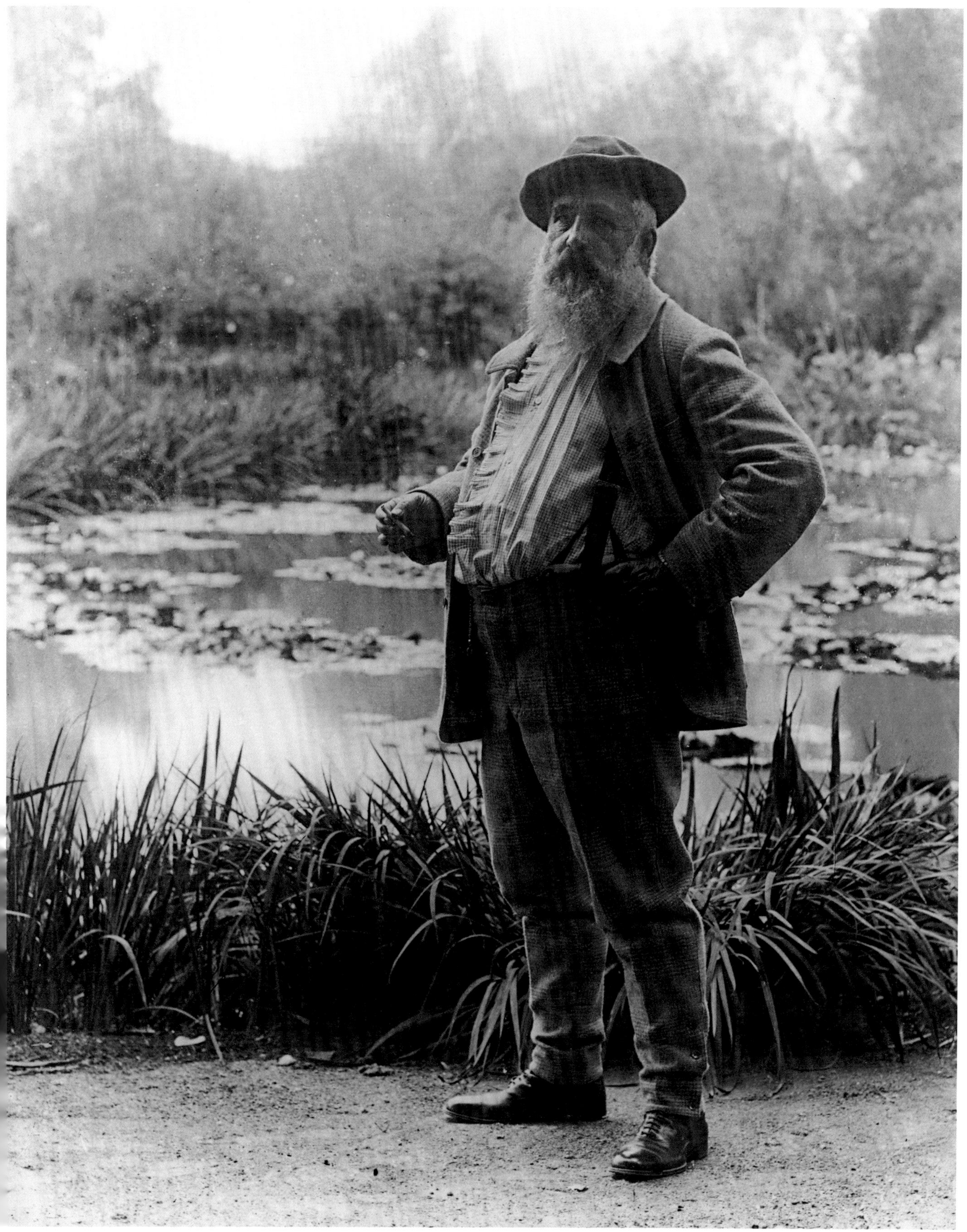

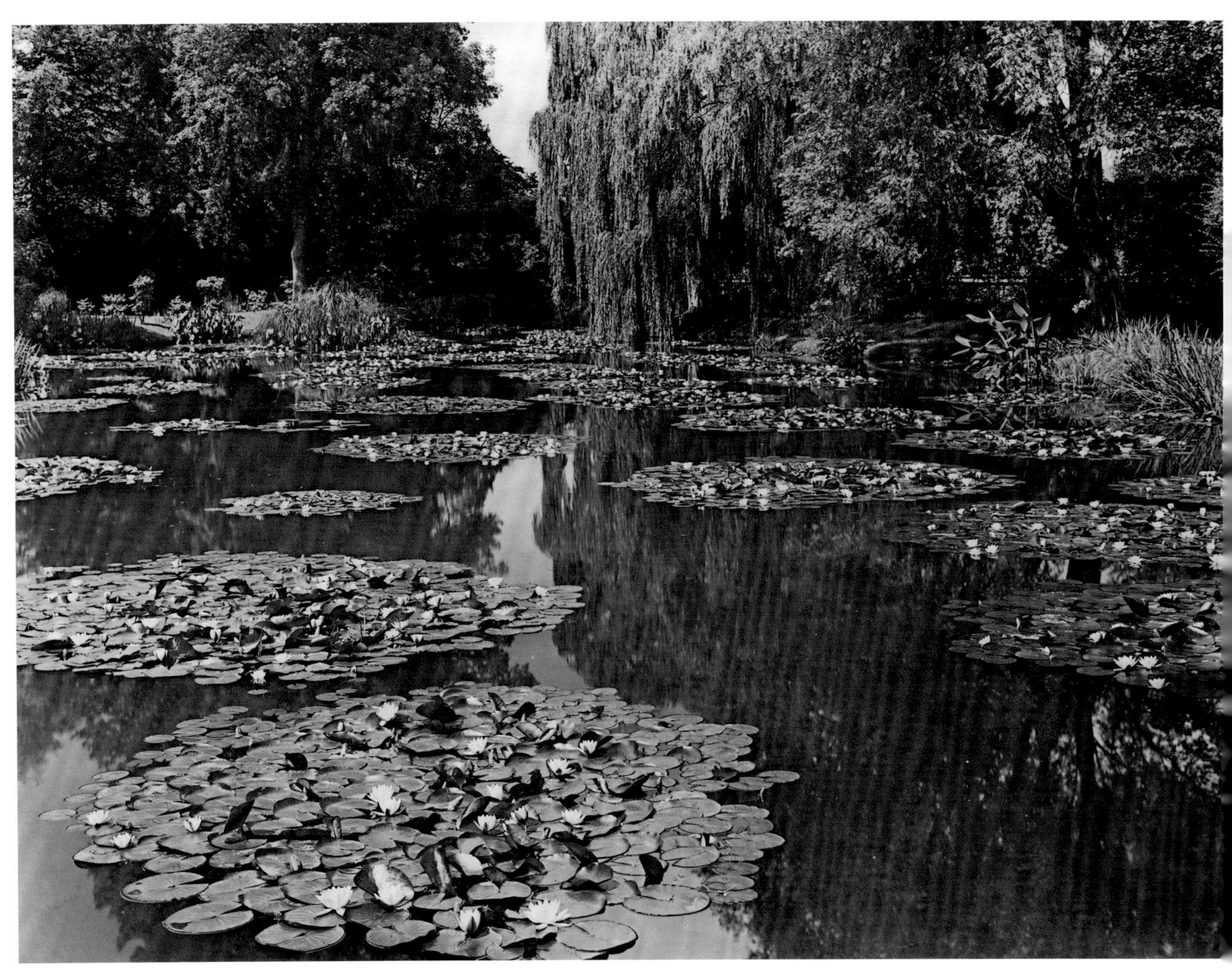

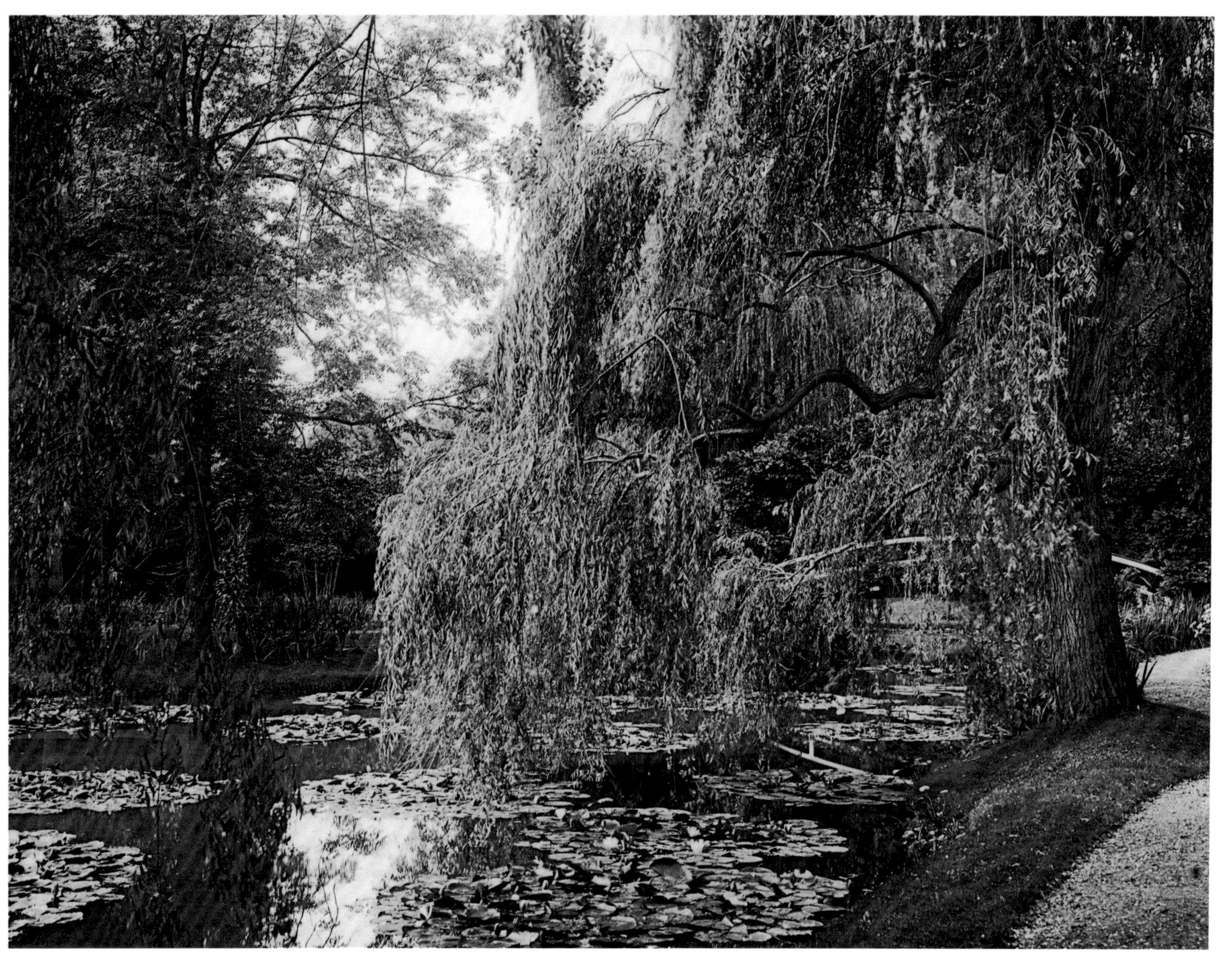

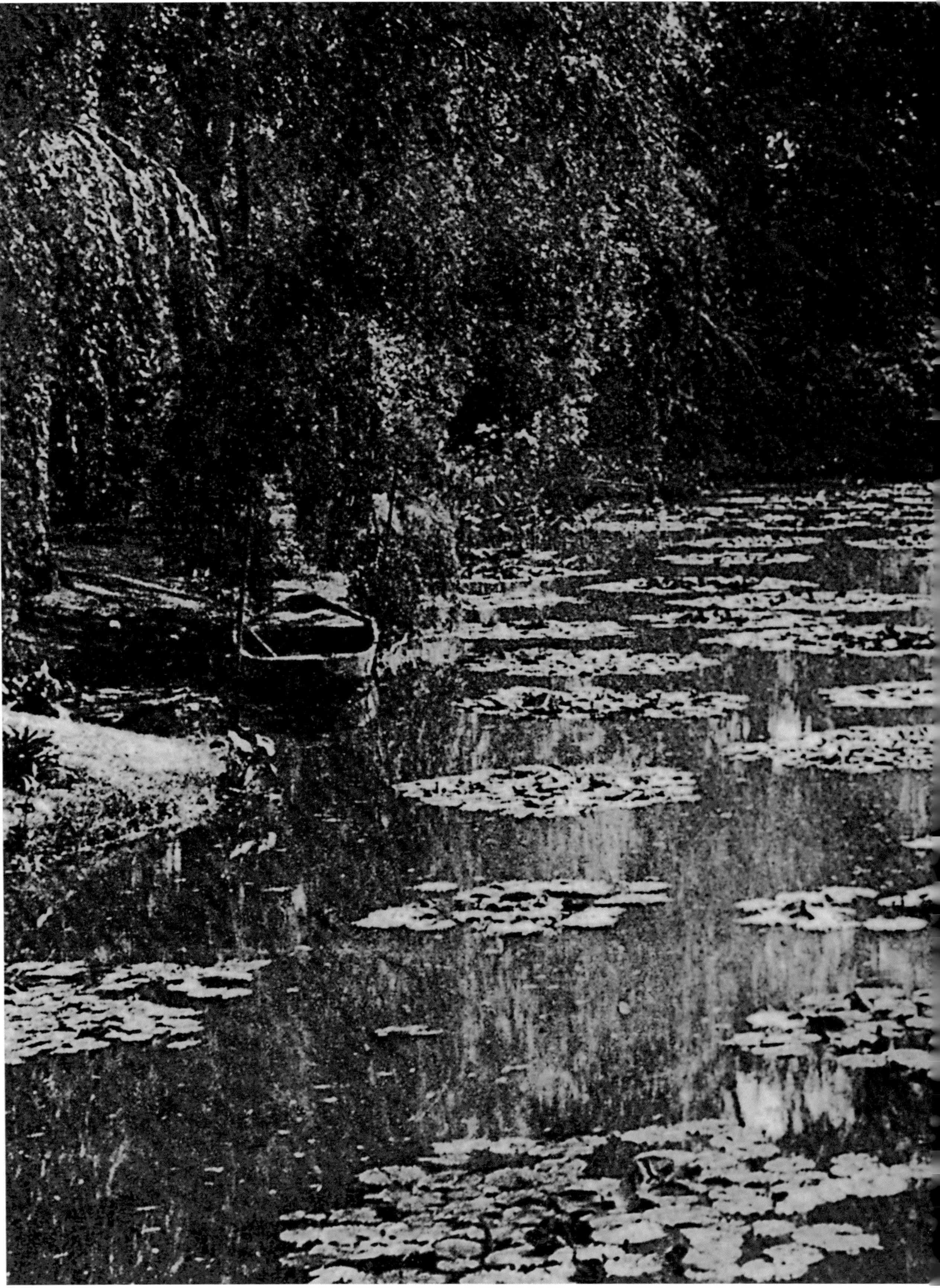

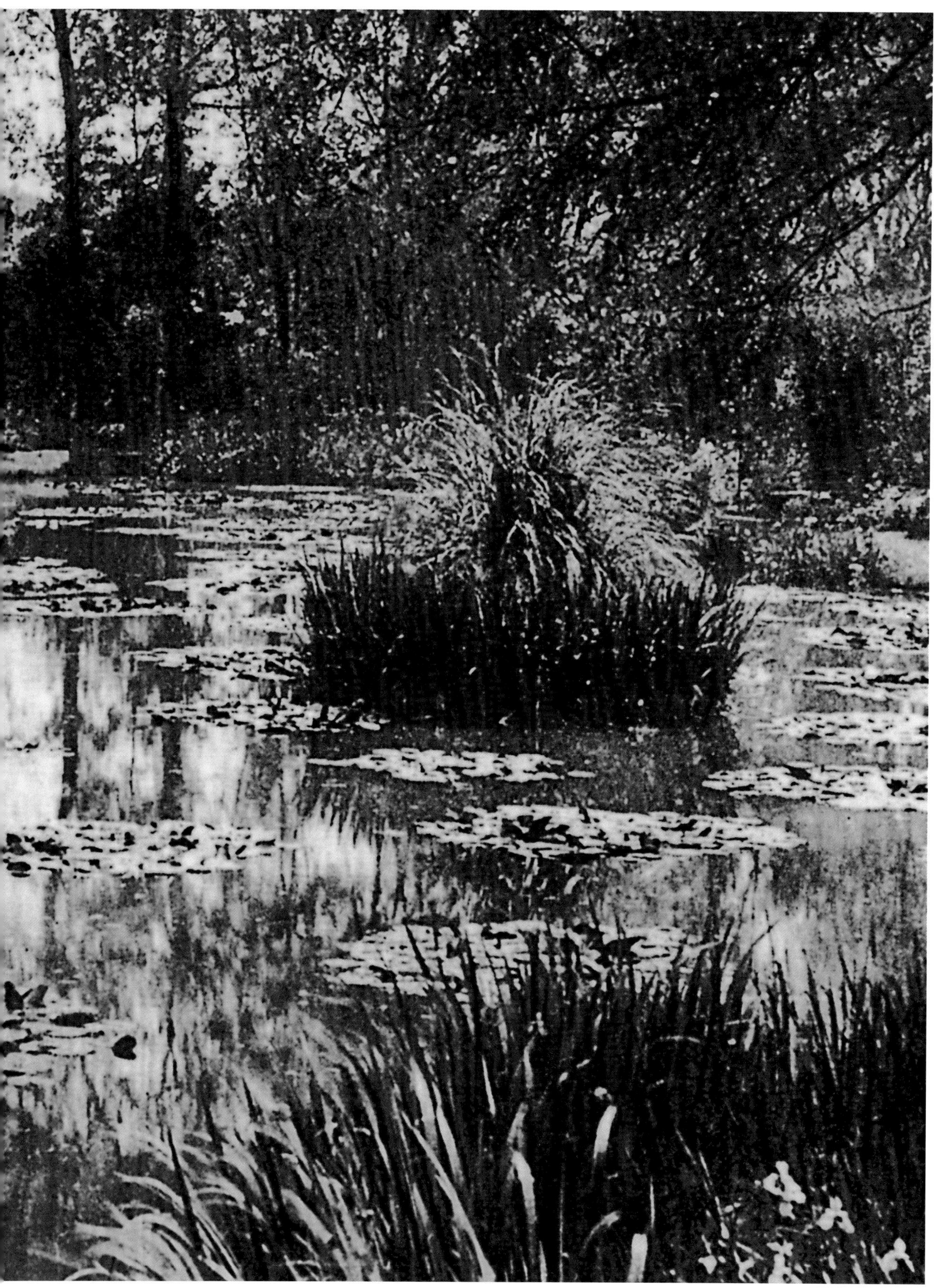

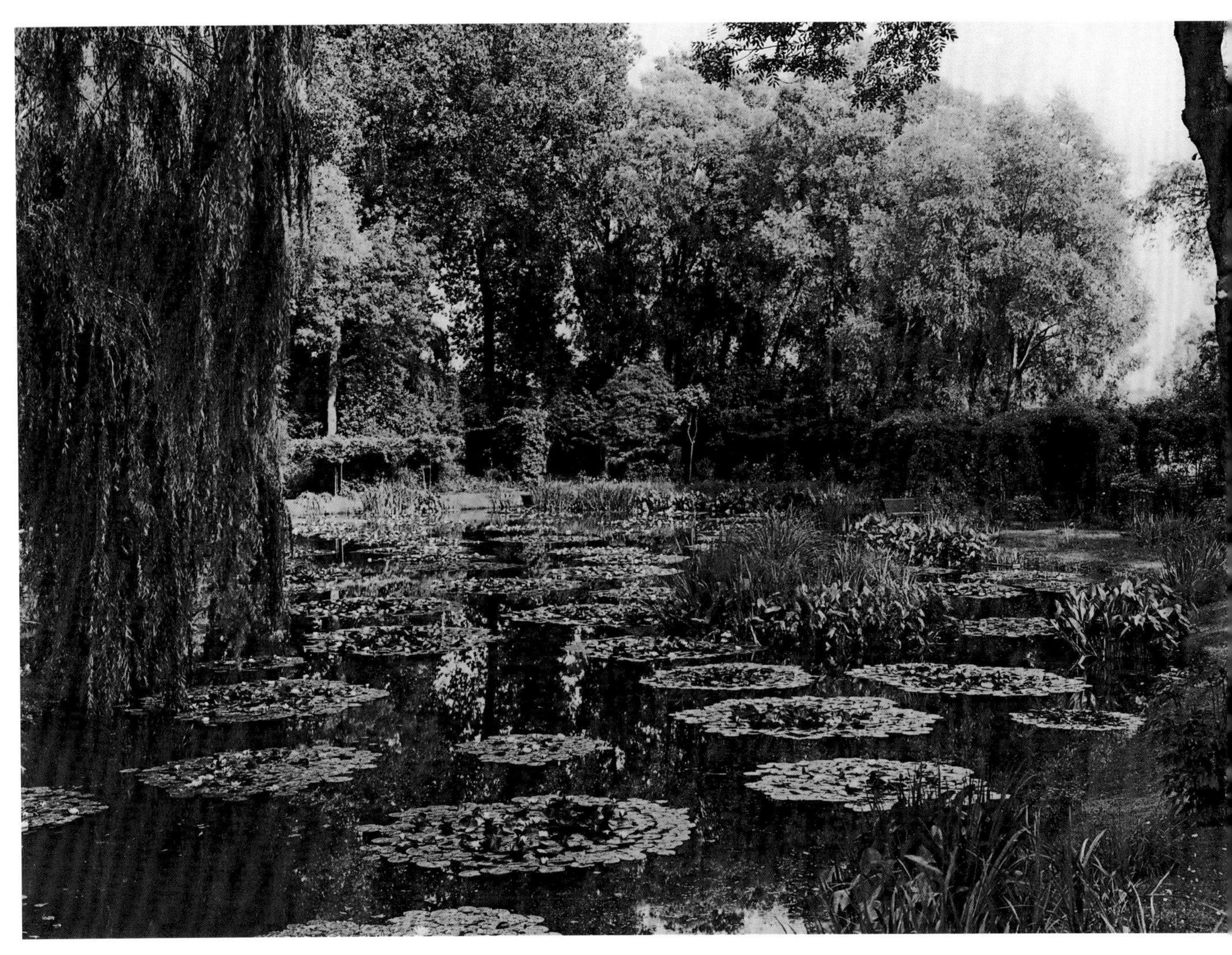

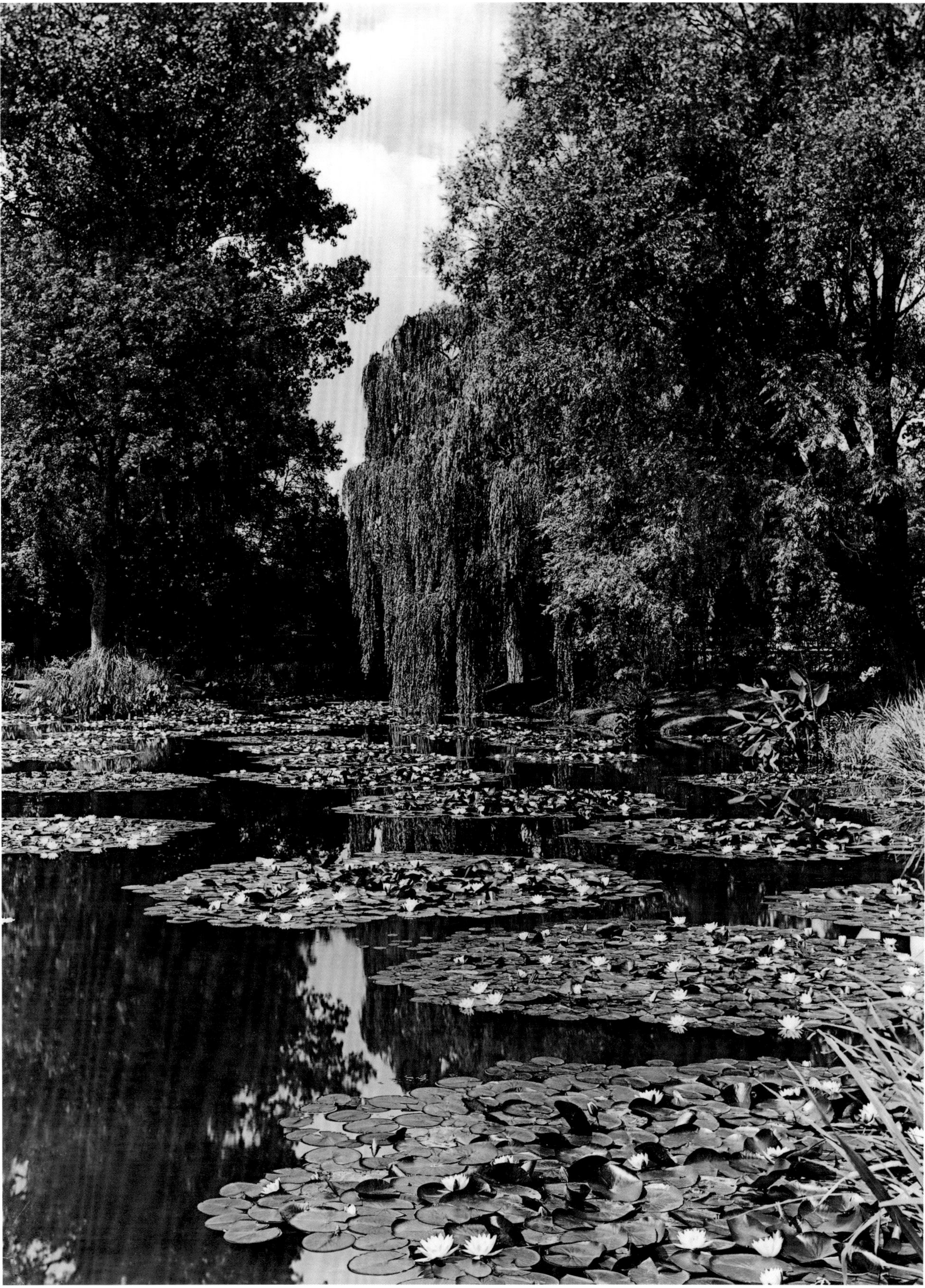

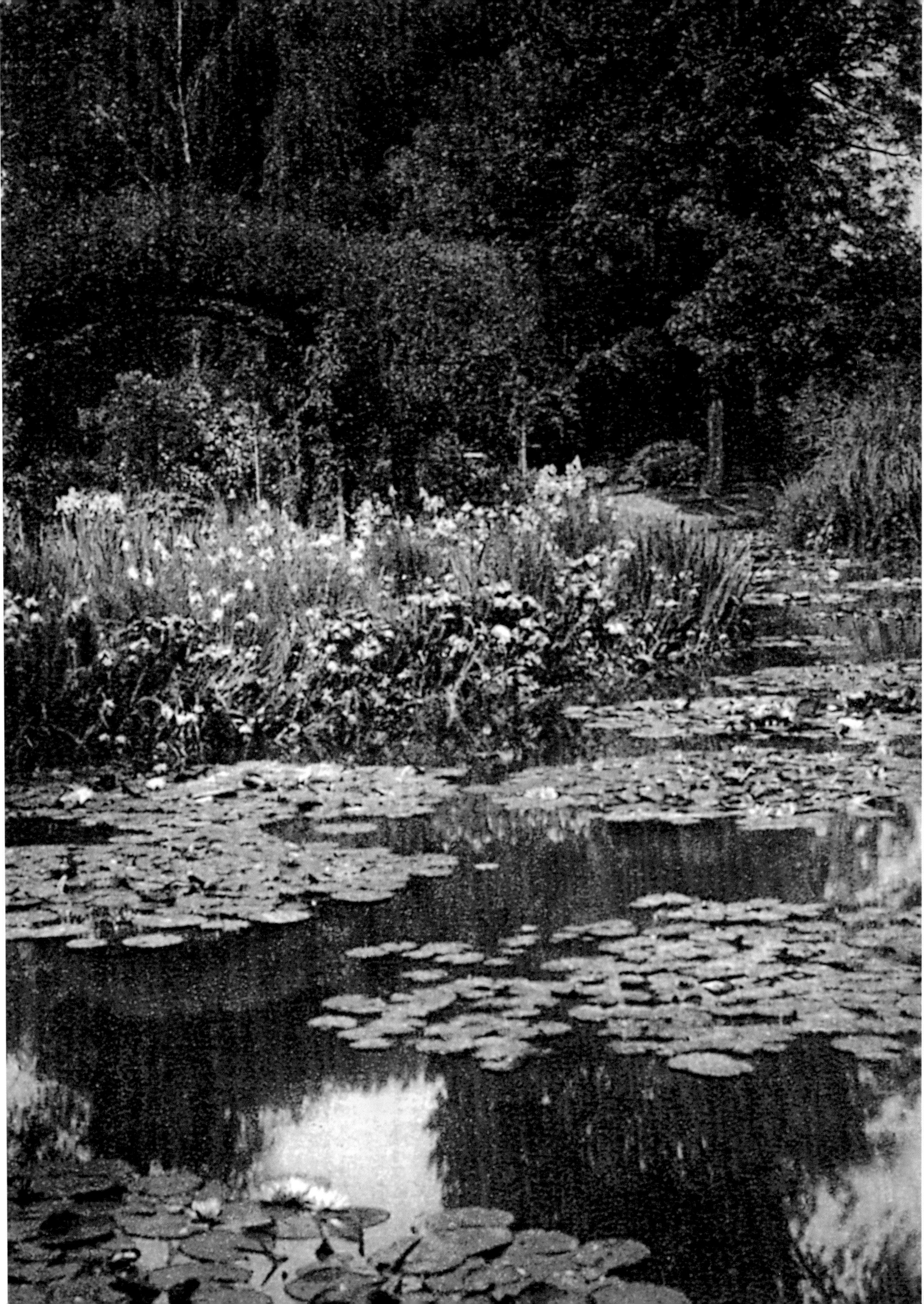

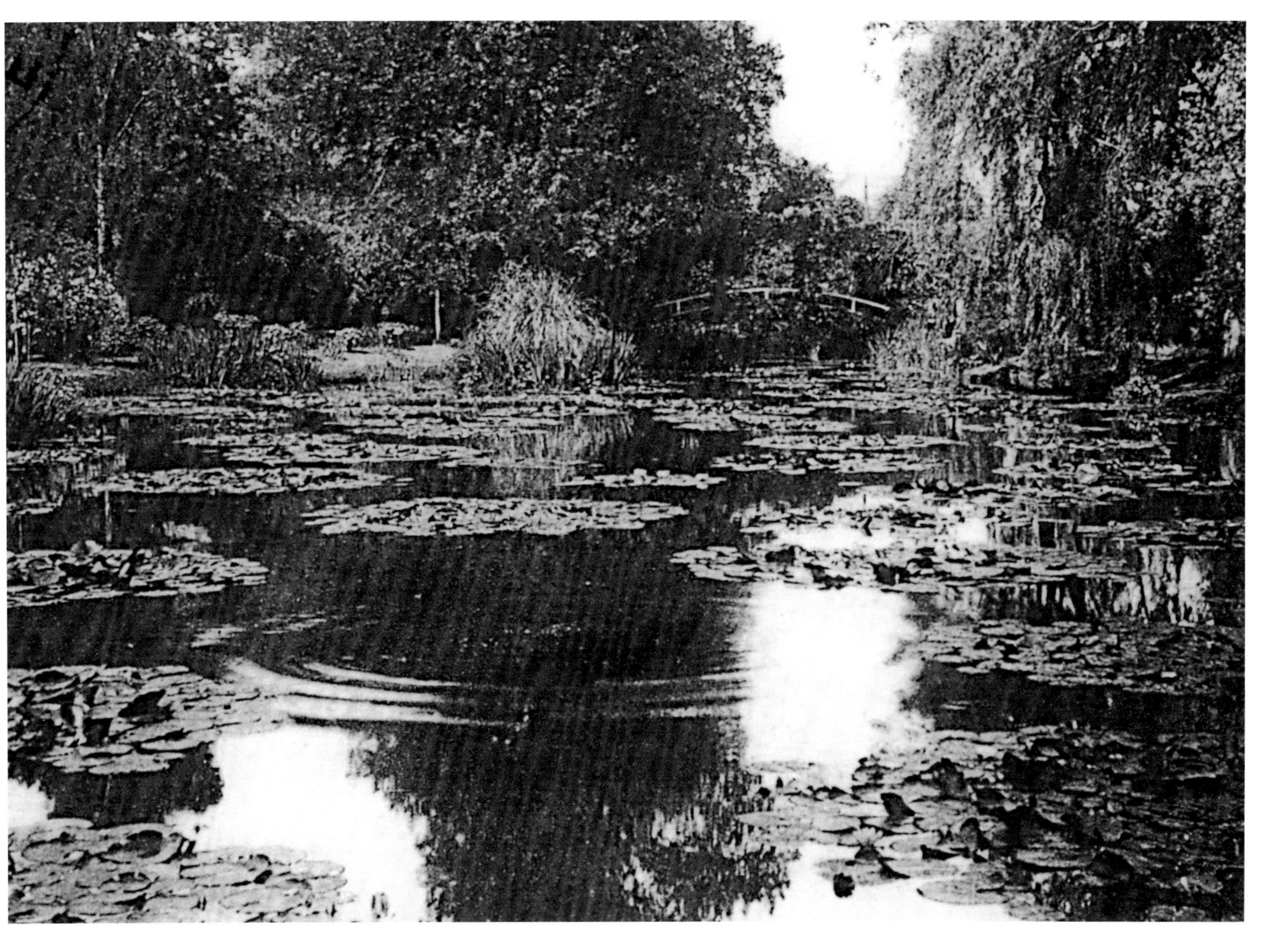

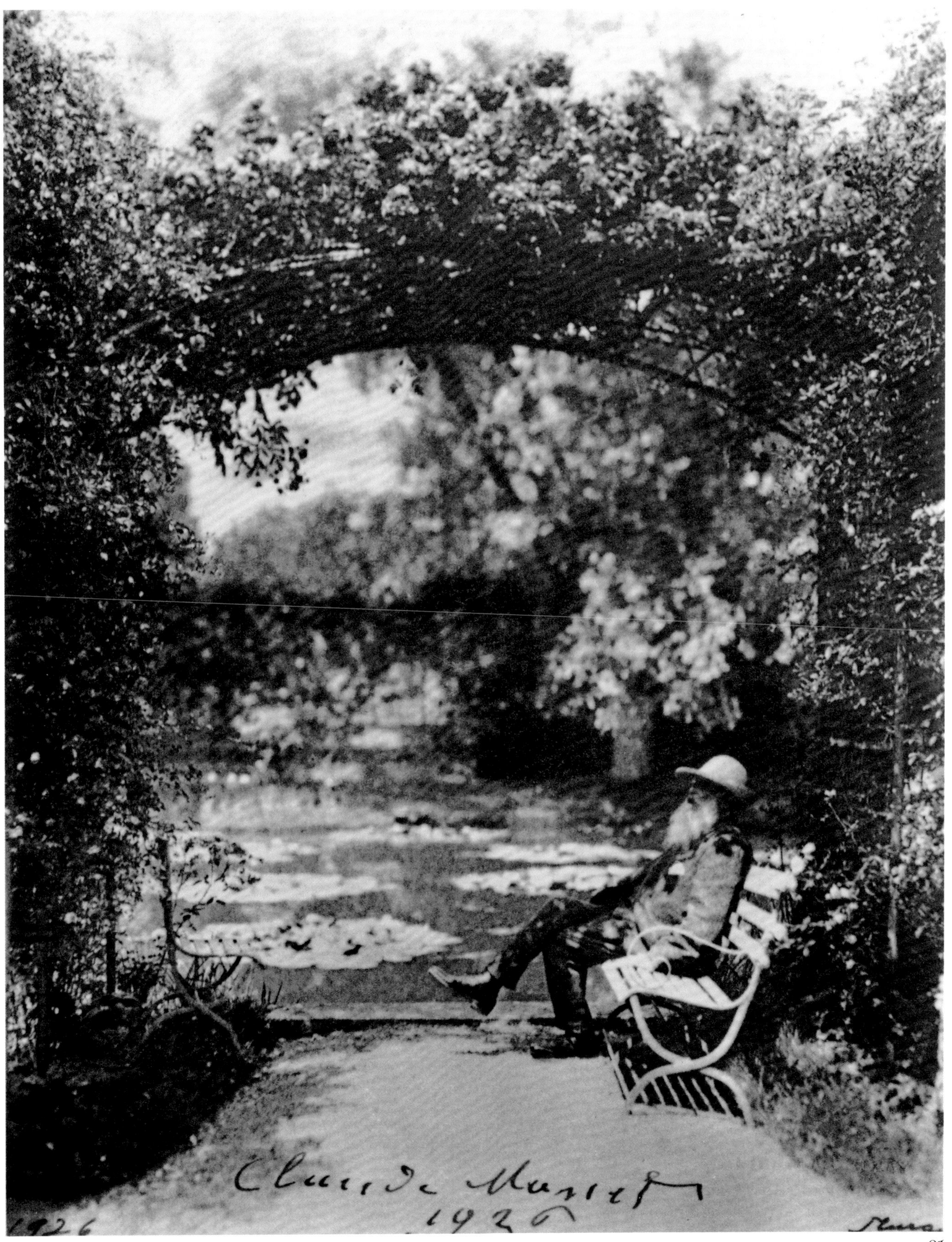
Claude Monet
1926
1926

Page 51	*Water Lilies*, 1905. Oil on canvas, 35 3/8 x 39 3/8 inches. Private collection. Photograph courtesy Acquavella Galleries, Inc., New York.
Page 53	*Water Lilies*, 1915. Oil on canvas, 58 5/8 x 78 3/4 inches. Musée Marmottan Monet, Paris. Bequest of Michel Monet.
Page 54	*Agapanthus I*, 1916–1917. Oil on canvas, 78 3/4 x 70 7/8 inches. Collection of The Museum of Modern Art, New York. Gift of Sylvia Slifka in memory of Joseph Slifka (donor retaining a life interest).
Page 55	*Iris*, circa 1922/1926. Oil on canvas, 78 3/4 x 79 1/8 inches. Collection of The Art Institute of Chicago. Art Institute Purchase Fund, 1956.1202. © The Art Institute of Chicago.
Pages 56–57	*Water Lilies*, 1917/1919. Oil on canvas 39 3/8 x 78 3/4 inches. Honolulu Academy of Arts. Purchased in memory of Robert Allerton, 1966 (3385.1).
Page 58	The water-lily pond and Japanese footbridge, early 1920s. Photograph by French school. Musée Marmottan Monet, Paris. Courtesy The Bridgeman Art Library International, Ltd.
Page 59 (top)	*The Roses*, 1925–1926. Oil on canvas, 51 3/16 x 78 3/4 inches. Musée Marmottan Monet, Paris. Courtesy The Bridgeman Art library International, Ltd.
Page 59 (bottom)	*The Irises*, 1924–1925. Oil on canvas, 41 3/4 x 61 inches. Musée Marmottan Monet, Paris. Courtesy The Bridgeman Art Library International, Ltd.
Page 60	*Flowers by the Pond (Les Hémérocalles)*, 1914–1917. Oil on canvas, 59 1/16 x 55 1/2 inches. Musée Marmottan Monet, Paris. Courtesy The Bridgeman Art Library International, Ltd.
Page 61	*White and Yellow Water Lilies*, 1914–1917. Oil on canvas, 78 3/4 x 78 3/4 inches. Kunstmuseum, Winterthur, Switzerland (813).
Pages 62–63	*The Japanese Bridge at Giverny*, circa 1923. Oil on canvas, 35 1/16 x 39 3/8 inches. Musée Marmottan Monet, Paris. Courtesy The Bridgeman Art Library International, Ltd.
Pages 64–65	*The Japanese Bridge*, 1918. Oil on canvas, 39 3/8 x 78 3/4 inches. Musée Marmottan Monet, Paris. Courtesy The Bridgeman Art Library International, Ltd.
Pages 66	*Water Lilies*, 1914/1917. Oil on canvas, 78 3/4 x 79 1/8 inches. Musée Marmottan Monet, Paris. Courtesy The Bridgeman Art Library International, Ltd.

Page 67 — Monet in the water-lily decoration studio, 1922. Photograph by H. B. Lachman. Private collection.

Page 68 — Portrait of Claude Monet by Baron de Meyer, 1905. Archives Durand-Ruel, Paris (photograph number 17295).

Page 69 — The garden at Giverny, 1914. Photograph by French school. Archives Larousse, Paris. Lauros / Giraudon / The Bridgeman Art Library International, Ltd.

Pages 70, 71 — The water-lily pond. Collection Georges Truffaut. Courtesy Société Clause.

Pages 72, 73 — The water-lily pond. From *Country Life*.

Page 74 — The garden at Giverny, 1914. Photograph by French school. Archives Larousse, Paris. Lauros / Giraudon / The Bridgeman Art Library International, Ltd.

Pages 75–77 — The water-lily pond. From *Country Life*.

Pages 78, 79 — The water-lily garden. Collection Georges Truffaut. Courtesy Société Clause.

Page 80 (top) — Georges Clemenceau and Claude Monet in the water garden at Giverny, 1921. Photograph by the Kuroki / Matsukata families.

Page 80 (bottom) — Madame Kuroki, Claude Monet, Alice Butler, Blanche Hoschedé-Monet, and Georges Clemenceau in the water garden at Giverny. Photograph by French school. Musée Marmottan Monet, Paris. Courtesy The Bridgeman Art Library International, Ltd.

Page 81 — Monet by the water-lily pond, circa 1904. Bulloz, Paris.

Page 82 — The water garden. From *Country Life*.

Page 83 — The water garden. Collection Georges Truffaut. Courtesy Société Clause.

Pages 84–85 — Postcard of the water garden.

Pages 86, 87 — The water-lily pond. From *Country Life*.

Pages 88, 89 — Postcards of the water-lily pond. Private collection.

Page 91 — Monet beneath flowering arches, 1926. Photograph by Nickolas Muray. Collection of The Museum of Modern Art, New York. Gift of Mrs. Nickolas Muray.